The Late Middle Ages

James Barter

LUCENT BOOKS

An imprint of Thomson Gale, a part of The Thomson Corporation

THOMSON

™

GALE

Detroit • New York • San Francisco • San Diego • New Haven, Conn. • Waterville, Maine • London • Munich

LIBRARY OF CONGRESS CATALOGING-IN-PUBLICATION DATA

Barter, James, 1946–
  The late Middle Ages / by James Barter.
    p. cm. — (World history series)
  Includes bibliographical references and index.
  ISBN 1-59018-654-0 (hard cover : alk. paper)
  1. Middle Ages—History. 2. Civilization, Medieval. 3. Europe—History—
476–1492. I. Title. II. Series.
D117.B32 2005
940.1—dc22

                                          2004029679

Printed in the United States of America

Contents

Foreword

Each year, on the first day of school, nearly every history teacher faces the task of explaining why his or her students should study history. Many reasons have been given. One is that lessons exist in the past from which contemporary society can benefit and learn. Another is that exploration of the past allows us to see the origins of our customs, ideas, and institutions. Concepts such as democracy, ethnic conflict, or even things as trivial as fashion or mores, have historical roots.

Reasons such as these impress few students, however. If anything, these explanations seem remote and dull to young minds. Yet history is anything but dull. And therein lies what is perhaps the most compelling reason for studying history: History is filled with great stories. The classic themes of literature and drama—love and sacrifice, hatred and revenge, injustice and betrayal, adversity and overcoming adversity—fill the pages of history books, feeding the imagination as well as any of the great works of fiction do.

The story of the Children's Crusade, for example, is one of the most tragic in history. In 1212 Crusader fever hit Europe. A call went out from the pope that all good Christians should journey to Jerusalem to drive out the hated Muslims and return the city to Christian control. Heeding the call, thousands of children made the jour-

ney. Parents bravely allowed many children to go, and entire communities were inspired by the faith of these small Crusaders. Unfortunately, many boarded ships captained by slave traders, who enthusiastically sold the children into slavery as soon as they arrived at their destination. Thousands died from disease, exposure, and starvation on the long march across Europe to the Mediterranean Sea. Others perished at sea.

Another story, from a modern and more familiar place, offers a soul-wrenching view of personal humiliation but also the ability to rise above it. Hatsuye Egami was one of 110,000 Japanese Americans sent to internment camps during World War II. "Since yesterday we Japanese have ceased to be human beings," he wrote in his diary. "We are numbers. We are no longer Egamis, but the number 23324. A tag with that number is on every trunk, suitcase and bag. Tags, also, on our breasts." Despite such dehumanizing treatment, most internees worked hard to control their bitterness. They created workable communities inside the camps and demonstrated again and again their loyalty as Americans.

These are but two of the many stories from history that can be found in the pages of the Lucent Books World History series. All World History titles rely on sound research and verifiable evidence, and all give students a clear sense of time, place, and chronology through maps and time-lines as well as text.

All titles include a wide range of author-itative perspectives that demonstrate the complexity of historical interpretation and sharpen the reader's critical thinking skills. Formally documented quotations and annotated bibliographies enable students to locate and evaluate sources, often instantaneously via the Internet, and serve as valuable tools for further research and debate.

Finally, Lucent's World History titles present rousing good stories, featuring vivid primary source quotations drawn from unique, sometimes obscure sources such as diaries, public records, and con-temporary chronicles. In this way, the voic-es of participants and witnesses as well as important biographers and historians bring the study of history to life. As we are caught up in the lives of others, we are reminded that we too are characters in the ongoing human saga, and we are better prepared for our own roles.

Important Dates in the

1066
William the Conqueror invades England.

1090
The Chinese invent the first water-powered mechanical clock.

1204
Crusaders sack the Byzantine Empire's capital city, Constantinople.

1174
Saladin conquers Syria.

1000	1050	1100	1150	1200

A.D.

1080
Spanish soldiers discover vast libraries when they invade Toledo, Spain.

1000
The Late Middle Ages begin.

1182
Philip II banishes the Jews from France.

1163
Construction begins on the cathedral of Notre Dame in Paris, France.

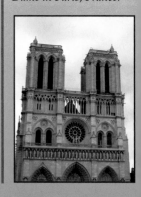

Late Middle Ages

1206
Genghis Khan
is declared
supreme ruler
of the Mongols.

1271
*Marco Polo embarks
on his first voyage to
China.*

1325
The Aztecs begin
building their capital,
Tenochtitlán, in what
is now Mexico.

1386
*English poet Geoffrey
Chaucer begins work on
his masterpiece,* The
Canterbury Tales.

1250   **1300**   **1350**   **1400**

1215
*The Magna Carta
is signed.*

1337
*The Hundred Years'
War breaks out
between England and
France.*

1347
The Black Death
(bubonic plague)
epidemic begins in
Europe.

1400
The Late Middle
Ages end.

Introduction

Gradual Awakenings

Around the year 1000, a variety of historical forces were set in motion that gradually reshaped European civilization. Initially barely perceptible and imperfectly understood by Europeans at the time, those forces combined over time and reached their zenith around 1400, recreating Europe and placing its civilization on the threshold of what historians today refer to as modern Europe.

Historians mark this four-hundred-year period as the Late Middle Ages—occasionally called the High Middle Ages—and recognize it as the time when many of the qualities present in modern Europe, and America as well, were first expressed in rudimentary forms. Among the concepts that emerged were autonomous nations, governments, the separation of church and state, international trade, equal application of the law, universities as centers of intellectual excellence, and great cities functioning as cultural, governmental, and commercial centers. The Late Middle Ages was

also the time when Europeans first considered themselves to be a single culture.

The main features of this new medieval civilization evolved out of the preceding five-hundred-year period that historians refer to as the Early Middle Ages. Essentially, the Late Middle Ages can be loosely characterized as a time of gradual awakenings after centuries of disorder. The first of these, an awakening to a vast world of economic and cultural possibilities, resulted from trade with the Middle East that followed the religious wars called the Crusades. Merchants and businessmen amassed huge fortunes, and the general population achieved greater prosperity. Newly minted gold coins stimulated the revival of old cities and the construction of new ones. Peasant children were free to

In this late medieval illustration, knights on horseback conquer the Spanish city of Pamplona from the Moors in the eleventh century.

break away from the dreary lives of their ancestors to seek work in cities, where life was more colorful and jobs more plentiful.

Amid the tempestuous swirl of economic and social change emerged an awakening about the human potential for better lives and brighter futures. The energy contained in this new movement called humanism was manifested in new forms of art and architecture, works of literature, and a nascent interest in science. This new sense of optimism, based on logic rather than the mysticism of the Catholic Church, challenged the authority of the popes and kings to direct people's lives.

By the fourteenth century, it was apparent that a new system of governance was needed to regulate a more complex and sophisticated Europe. Kings and popes awakened to the reality that their absolute authority would no longer be tolerated. Fearing for their futures, kings agreed to limit their authority and abide by written laws fairly and evenly applied. By the fifteenth century, nation-states, the precursors to modern democratic nations, had begun to emerge. Yet, not all nations experienced the Late Middle Ages in the same way or at the same pace.

The Patchwork of Medieval Europe

No aspect of the Late Middle Ages, whether working conditions, village life,

In this medieval manuscript illumination, a man studies the planets. The Late Middle Ages witnessed the birth of science in Europe.

personal relationships, spiritual beliefs, or physical surroundings, was the same everywhere. Vikings living in Sweden overlooking ice-covered fjords, for example, had a very different sense of the times than did Sicilian farmers tilling their red clay fields overlooking the warm, translucent Mediterranean waters.

Great distances combined with slow or nonexistent communications conspired to create a multitude of experiences for Europeans. Although historians speak in general terms about life during the Late Middle Ages, little of the homogeneity common to modern cultures existed. Nations bordering the Mediterranean Sea were heavily influenced by local traditions deriving from the Roman Empire, whereas northern Scandinavian nations, untouched by Roman legions, followed tribal customs. Island nations, such as England, Scotland, Wales, Ireland, and Iceland, developed still different experiences because of their watery isolation. In the view of historian Thomas Asbridge, "Their [Europeans'] world was a patchwork of villages and emerging towns with no unifying concept of country or even Europe."[1]

All villagers shared general historical experiences but not necessarily personal ones. Germans living in Saxony lived on a diet of turnips, heavy barley breads, and dry salted gristle, while Frenchmen in Brittany enjoyed an assortment of seafood with rich dairy products and local wines. Italians living in major seaports suffered deadly diseases carried by foreign freighters, while citizens of Prague or Vienna experienced relatively few. Wars leapfrogged across provinces, obliterating some villages and inexplicably leaving others unscathed. And depending on local conditions, some peasants died trying to escape to a better life, yet others found contentment in their villages.

Despite their differences, however, medieval societies had one scourge in common: incessant warfare. Before any of the achievements of the Late Middle Ages could be realized, the fundamental problem of recapturing peace and a sense of security was of paramount importance around the year 1000. To accomplish that objective, medieval society required a restructuring.

Chapter One

The Advent of Feudal Society

The transformation that began the Late Middle Ages around the year 1000 grew out of the preceding five hundred years known as the Early Middle Ages. This period can loosely be characterized as a self-protective reaction to the collapse of the Roman Empire in approximately 500. For hundreds of years before that historical event, Rome had unified most of Europe by applying a single justice system, military, language, and currency. Although Europeans were tightly dominated by Romans, they prospered under relatively peaceful and stable conditions. Immediately following Rome's collapse, however, Europe plunged into a state of disorder.

Staggering from violent foreign invasions, internal lawlessness, and economic stagnation, political and spiritual leaders struggled to restore order. For nearly five hundred years a variety of leaders and movements tried unsuccessfully to recapture the security and balance that Rome had once provided. Nearly everything about the Early Middle Ages reflected makeshift adjustments to conditions that were constantly unraveling. The worst was a flurry of invasions by marauding tribes such as the Vandals, Ostrogoths, Huns, and Visigoths, who collectively plundered crops and livestock while looting cities of everything that could be carried off and killing thousands who dared to oppose them.

The response on the part of Europeans to this terror was to hide. They built great stone walls around castles and even around entire cities for protection. Then, when invaders arrived, everyone fled behind the wall, shut the gates, and fought until they fended off the enemy, bribed them to go elsewhere, or perished.

Marauding Germanic tribes make landfall in Britain in this twelfth-century painting. Throughout the Early Middle Ages, Europe was plagued by invading tribes.

Charlemagne

Charlemagne, meaning "Charles the Great" in the early French language, was born in 742 to King Pepin the Short. Little is known of his childhood but when Pepin died in 768, he specified in his will that his kingdom be divided equally between Charlemagne and his brother Carolman. When Carolman died three years later and divided his kingdom between his sons, Charlemagne murdered his nephews and seized their territories.

For the next thirty years, Charlemagne engaged in continuous wars of aggression that extended his empire deep into Germany, northern Spain, and parts of Italy. By the end of the eighth century, Charlemagne was the most powerful monarch in Europe, and in 800 the pope crowned him emperor of the Holy Roman Empire.

Following his territorial gains, Charlemagne applied himself to administering his vast kingdom. He understood the need to delegate authority over his many provinces to worthy nobles. He also knew that the various people he had brought together in one nation were from different ethnic groups, and he allowed each group to retain its own laws in local areas. To ensure justice, he saw to it that each group's laws were set down in writing and carefully enforced and that the nobility treated the peasantry in a fair manner.

When the Late Middle Ages declined and modern Europe emerged, many European kings looked back to Charlemagne's rule for examples they could follow of how he administered his nation. The legacy Charlemagne left them was a commitment to autonomy for his subjects, reasonable laws, a dedication to education, and restrictions placed on the authority of the nobility.

During this grim period, a general malaise descended over Europe. Paul the Deacon, an eighth-century French historian, noted the wide-ranging depression as he described his ride from Carcassonne to Paris:

The flocks remain alone in the pastures. You saw villas or fortified places filled with people in utter silence. The whole world seemed brought to its ancient stillness: no voice in the field, no whistling of shepherds. The harvests were untouched. Human habitations became the abode of wild beasts.[2]

Gone were the great cities of the Roman Empire. With the exception of a few major commercial centers such as Bruges, Budapest, London, Belgrade, Marseilles, and Paris, most shrank to small towns, and a few disappeared altogether. Even Rome, which once boasted a population of 1 million, had become little more than a squatter's camp with sheep grazing where the senate once met. Central governments that once confidently dispensed justice collapsed, and famed schools and libraries closed their doors. Within the chaos of the Early Middle Ages, long-distance trade ceased as paved Roman roads, once the pride of the Roman Empire, deteriorated to rutted dirt paths plagued by brigands. With only one notable but short-lived exception, that of King Charlemagne during the early ninth century, no leader possessed the administrative abilities or farsightedness to return Europe to the sense of order and normalcy enjoyed under the Romans.

The Emergence of the Late Middle Ages

Amid the general disorder, Europeans desperately sought any system capable of providing a stable economy and protection from the incessant foreign and regional invasions. The solution to those twin challenges was realized when individual local leaders stepped forth promising to defend entire villages of peasant farmers in exchange for a percentage of their crops and personal services. With a simple handshake and verbal pledge, leaders and farmers stumbled upon the relatively rudimentary political system that later historians called feudalism. At a time when kings could not be counted on to rule effectively, this system took hold. The relatively uncomplicated concept forged a contract between individuals and evolved into a system that encompassed all Europeans from mighty kings who autocratically ruled Europe's nations to ordinary peasants.

Exactly how and where feudalism began remains a mystery, yet historians

During his reign as Holy Roman emperor, Charlemagne organized a centralized system of government to administer his far-flung realms.

Feudal Europe

As Europe emerged from the chaos of the Early Middle Ages, a feudal system of governing developed. Europe became divided into regions that were governed by feudal lords, yet the boundaries changed many times in the course of the Middle Ages.

FINNS

NORWAY

SWEDEN

Baltic Sea

SCOTLAND

North Sea

Irish Kingdoms and Chiefdoms

DENMARK

Lithuanians

RUSSIAN STATES

Welsh Principalities

ENGLAND

POLAND

Saxony

Thuringia

BOHEMIA

GERMANY

Normandy

Swabia

Bavaria

HUNGARY

Cumins (Turkic)

FRANCE

Carinthia

Anjou

NAVARRE

Aquitaine

COUNTY OF TOULOUSE

KINGDOM OF ITALY

Black Sea

LEON

BYZANTINE EMPIRE

PORTUGAL

CASTILLE

ARAGON

PAPAL STATES

EMIRATE OF MALLORCA

ALMOHAD CALIPHATE

KINGDOM OF SICILY

Mediterranean Sea

generally agree that the seeds of feudalism took root independently in many towns and villages across Europe within one to two generations. Initially it was probably a spur-of-the-moment experiment tried in a few places, and once it proved to be better than chaos, it gradually spread to neighboring villages. Within a hundred years, it dominated Europe.

Once feudalism took hold, improvements in people's lives followed. An economic system unfolded that provided for most people's needs for food, shelter, clothing, and other basic necessities. Improvements, however, were not evenly distributed across the population. The wealthy enjoyed more than most, while many poor families struggled to eke out a meager existence. Nonetheless, as rudimentary local commerce returned, towns once again began to flourish and a semblance of order was restored in the form of primitive local laws and court systems.

Feudalism

At the heart of the feudal system was the quest for protection and security. The many violent invasions that washed across Europe interrupted normal communications and travel. Kings feared traveling the roads between Paris and Bordeaux, London and Northumberland, Frankfurt and Hamburg, or Stockholm and Gothenburg. Local self-sufficiency had to develop for farmers, fishermen, and craftsmen to survive. Europe's rural society, which made up 90 to 95 percent of the population, organized so that each of thousands of hamlets could survive on its own resources.

Farmers needing assistance protecting their property and families formed a relationship with a more powerful man who was wealthy enough to own land, weapons, and a warhorse. Warring men agreed to protect peasants and to lease them land in exchange for compensation. At a time when money did not exist, compensation was offered in the form of either goods such as food, household items, and construction material or services such as chopping firewood, shoeing horses, and sewing clothes. Any man who pledged to provide protection to others took the informal title of "lord," and anyone seeking leased land and protection was called a vassal. Many kings encouraged the peasantry to form feudal relationships with armed lords, as this eleventh-century French document indicates: "We wish that every free man in our kingdom select the lord whom he prefers."[3]

The relationship that shaped feudalism was loyalty between a vassal and his or her lord. Powerful lords organized armies and built manor homes surrounded by great stone walls to protect their families as well as entire populations of farmers and craftsmen in times of invasion. Some of these manor homes were relatively simple fortified houses, but many more were elaborate stone castles ringed with stone walls and protected by drawbridges and deep moats filled with water. Jean de Colmieu described the typical castle of twelfth-century northern France this way:

It is the custom of the nobles to make a mound of earth as high as possible and then encircle it with a moat as wide and deep as possible. They enclose the space on top with a palisade of very strong hewn logs firmly fixed together or with several thicknesses of mortared stone strengthened at intervals by towers. Within the walls is a house and central citadel which commands the whole circuit of the defense. The entrance is across a bridge . . . supported on posts . . . crossing the moat.[4]

Providing protection increased the authority of lords. Kings bestowed special privileges on lords and granted them the free use of the king's land in return for the use of the lords' armies to fight against other kings or to repel large invading forces. Kings also recognized that in addition to protecting their vassals, lords could be called upon to provide their villagers with primitive judicial systems and economic stability. As a reward for their contributions to local administration and military assistance, kings elevated lords and their families to the status of nobility, a rank that the peasant population could never attain.

Military skills created the nobility, and kept it in power. By the beginning of the twelfth century, the nobility, headed by the king, controlled all local and national affairs. Historian Norman Cantor stresses this point:

> Whatever else the aristocracy [nobility] did—in politics, religion, art, and literature—it was military valor and personal strength and courage that had originally made the great noble families powerful in society, and this phys-

ical prowess was continually necessary to sustain their position in society.[5]

The bond between lord and vassal was the essential component that held feudal society together. So important was the bond that a contract was required between the two parties specifying their relationship and what each owed to the other.

Paying Homage and Fealty

The private agreements that formed the feudal network of mutual services were called contracts of homage and fealty. The word *homage*, from the French word meaning "man" and sometimes "servant," referred to the lower-status member of the contract, and *fealty* meant to remain faithful. Contracts of homage and fealty applied to all levels of feudal society— kings and their immediate nobility as well as the nobility and the peasantry.

Contracts between kings and nobility were simple and consistently the same: Nobles provided kings with mounted knights in times of war. One eleventh-century French document records the Duke of Coucey annually owing the king thirty knights, the Duke of Anjou thirty-four, the Duke of Brittany thirty-six, and the Count of Flanders forty-seven.

In contracts between a village lord and his peasants, the lord promised to provide military protection and the use of his personal residence as a place of refuge in the event of an invasion. One thirteenth-century German contract between a lord and a peasant expresses the lord's obligation to protect and add a man to his group of protected vassals:

It is right that those who offer to us unbroken fidelity should be protected by our aid. And since such a faithful one of ours, by the favor of God, coming here in our palace, we willingly bear arms for those who have seen fit to swear trust and fidelity to us in our hand.[6]

What vassals agreed to provide depended on their skills and the needs of the lord.

Noblemen present a portion of their tax revenues to the king as part of their feudal obligations.

Farmers typically owed food of one sort or another. Contracts often specified an annual delivery of some quantity of wheat, sometimes a lamb, or monthly deliveries of cheese, eggs, and butter. Village craftsmen were expected to provide goods that they produced. Bakers provided the lord's daily bread, the cobbler made a specified number of pairs

of shoes, and the blacksmith repaired broken iron tools and shod the lord's horses. The carpenter might be required to work ten days a year repairing the lord's manor house.

Each party understood the terms of the contract, but that did not prevent many lords from demanding even more. Anger and resentment often erupted in villages when peasants were called from their family Christmas dinners to help prepare and serve the lord's dinner. Similar unreasonable demands beyond the scope of feudal contracts instilled bitterness in field hands when lords hosted hunting parties or weddings and required the vassals to provide, prepare, and serve food for the elaborate banquets.

By the twelfth century, thousands of feudal contracts defined European society. Although each country had its unique characteristics, all followed a similar model. Feudal contracts clearly defined two social classes, the nobility and the peasantry. Yet there was also a third that was regarded as distinct from the other two—the clergy, those who prayed.

Those Who Pray

The hold that the church exercised on everyone's life, both the material and spiritual, was profound. After the collapse of the Roman Empire, the practice of Christianity was one of the few experiences shared by everyone. As such, it functioned as a spiritual and cultural bond that held together two very distinct classes of people.

The church of the Late Middle Ages was the best organized and most powerful institution at that time. It was also the only one to reach out and embrace all of Europe. It was the one constant, as noted by historian Barbara Tuchman:

> Christianity was the matrix of medieval life: even cooking instructions called for boiling an egg "during the length of time wherein you say a Miserere [a psalm]." It governed birth, marriage, and death, sex, and eating, made the rules for law and medicine, gave philosophy and scholarship their subject matter. Membership in the Church was not a matter of choice; it was compul-

Vassals shear sheep and harvest wheat in the shadow of their lord's manor. A portion of their bounty would go as payment to their lord.

sory and without alternative, which gave it a hold not easy to dislodge.[7]

The church was the focus of village life. Most of the important life events were celebrated within the churchyard. The parish priest knew every family member and the problems each endured. His principal duties were to administer the sacraments when needed. Each villager, regardless of social position, received from him the sacrament of baptism, absolution of sins following confession, marriage for those who chose to marry, last rites before dying, and final prayers at grave sites.

The church also buoyed the spirits of the dispossessed. At a time when poverty, hunger, deadly diseases, war, and high infant mortality rates made life almost unbearable, the church promised a better life in the afterworld. To the medieval mind, the quality of one's spiritual life and focus on attaining the kingdom of heaven were more important than life's concerns and suffering here on earth. The church also provided mystical explanations for all of life's unsolved mysteries and tended to support the nobles in their supremacy over the peasant class.

It also fell to the clergy to justify many of life's apparent injustices. One of the most often cited by the peasantry was the lack of

A medieval Italian panel depicts the Madonna holding the infant Jesus. Christian belief was dominant in medieval Europe.

Vassals plant vines and harvest grapes as their lord looks on. Medieval society was based on an extremely rigid class system.

class mobility. With the exception of the clergy, family determined everyone's class from cradle to grave. Only on a few rare occasions might a peasant who had displayed notable military courage receive the title of nobility. Class also determined marriages. A marriage outside of one's class was rare. Nobles condemned marriages with the peasantry, fearing it would lower their social standing in the view of neighboring nobles and because it might disrupt the inheritance of land and family fortune. This static social system was justified in many ways, such as this one from a twelfth-century cleric who points to God as its architect:

God himself has willed that among men, some must be lords and some serfs [vassals], in such a fashion that the lords venerate and love God, and that the serfs love and venerate their lord following the word of the Apostle; serfs obey your temporal lords with fear and trembling; lords treat your serfs according to justice and equity.[8]

One's class, more than any other factor, also determined a family's wealth, or lack of it. The feudal social structure that determined family economics applied to village economics as well. The feudal economy, like feudalism itself, was tied to the land and to those who controlled it.

Manorialism: The Feudal Economy

The feudal economy, referred to by historians as manorialism, derives its name from the lord's manor, which included his home and all landscape features such as streams, ponds, roads, bridges, buildings, forests, cropland, and pastures. The system was based on village agriculture. Manorialism, like feudalism, mainly applied to agrarian society rather than to major cities.

The manorial system was aimed at self-sufficiency for each village. The financial hallmark of the manorial system was the small plots of land, three to ten acres, that each peasant family tilled. Each family supported itself with the crops it could grow and supplemented them by trapping small game, tending vegetable patches, and raising small animals such as geese, chickens, and rabbits.

Peasants traded surplus crops and dairy products for other necessities. Without coinage, peasants traded food with village craftsmen for clothing, shoes, cooking pots, furniture, and a variety of other goods. In this way, the simple manorial system provided nearly everyone with

Peasant workers reap grain under their lord's watchful eye. The economy of the Late Middle Ages was largely dependent on agriculture.

life's necessities, but little else, especially for the families of peasant farmers who enjoyed only modest necessities even in the best of times. Glass for windows, for example, was a luxury few could afford, as were iron nails for building houses and sugar for cooking.

Since agriculture was the backbone of the economy, any crop failures rippled throughout the village, devastating everyone's livelihood. Invading armies, droughts, floods, and pestilence that destroyed the crops in turn destroyed the remainder of the economy. During times of hardship, lords reduced the goods and services owed them until farmers could recover. Thus, all suffered during hard times, but not to the same extent.

The village lord's primary role in manorialism was to ensure that the economy was balanced. He determined how much land was tilled, by whom, and what was planted. He also administered the sharing of draft animals for pulling plows and wagons. The responsibility for building communal structures such as bridges and mills for grinding grain fell to him as well. Each medieval manor looked different from all others, but the one characteristic that they all shared was a balanced economy.

Strict Laws Governing the Harvest

Crops were the backbone of the economy during the later Middle Ages. Because of their importance, there were numerous laws regulating them. The following four laws represent medieval concerns about destroying, stealing, and harvesting crops. They can be found in Judith Herrin's book A Medieval Miscellany.

If a man gathers in the fruits of his vineyard and brings in his beasts while the fruits of some plots are still ungathered, let him receive thirty lashes and make good the damage to the party injured.

If a man is found in a granary stealing corn, let him receive in the first place a hundred lashes, and make good the damage to the owner; if he is convicted a second time, let him pay twofold damages for his theft; if a third time, let him be blinded.

Let those who enter another man's furrows at harvest time and cut bundles or ears of corn be whipped and stripped of their shirts. Where people enter another man's vineyard or figyard, if they come to eat, let them go unpunished; if they are there to steal, let them be beaten, and stripped of their shirts.

If a farmer who is too poor to work his own vineyard takes flight and goes abroad, let those from whom claims are made by the public treasury gather in the grapes, and the farmer if he returns shall not be entitled to sue them for the wine.

Balance also depended on justice. Without the enforcement of laws and a penal code for punishing offenders, a village's economy and social structure crumbled. As he did with so much else, the lord assumed the responsibility for overseeing feudal justice for the well-being of the entire manor.

Feudal Justice

The lack of a viable central government meant that most feudal justice was practiced at the local level in small towns and villages. Although kings passed some laws applicable to the entire kingdom, such as laws governing taxation, disputes between cities, rights regulating the nobility, and the ownership and use of land, most people knew only local laws promulgated by their lords.

Local laws were rarely written down because few people could read or write. Consequently, laws were only vaguely known, and most were based on legend and custom. Children learned about laws by observing their parents. Most laws prescribed a variety of penalties for offenses such as theft, murder, drunkenness, trespassing, vandalism, assault, and illegal business practices.

In some villages, a manorial court under the jurisdiction of the lord oversaw all charges of local criminal behavior. The lord of the manor or a jury of peasant peers ultimately resolved all cases. Those involved addressed the lord or jury and made their accusations and defenses. After everyone had been heard, a judgment was rendered that could not be appealed. If someone was found guilty, punishment was also

This woodcut depicts four lawbreakers bound in a pillory and put on public display.

prescribed. One complaint about justice commonly heard at the village markets was that the lord and his family always managed to escape the law regardless of their culpability.

Prisons did not exist in medieval villages, so villagers dealt with offenders in a variety of other ways. One of the most common forms of punishment was clamping the criminal in the public pillory and inflicting physical pain. The pillory was a wood apparatus that secured the person's neck and hands to prevent him or her from escaping. Each village had a central public location where the pillory was placed.

The pillory was not only physically uncomfortable but a tool for humiliation. Petty thieves caught stealing at the marketplace, pickpockets working a Sunday crowd, or merchants caught cheating the public could expect to spend a day in one. Documents from the Late Middle Ages describe bakers constrained in the pillory with a loaf of bread hanging around their necks for adding sawdust to the dough. Butchers convicted of selling rotten meat were locked down for the day with smelly spoiled meat smeared over their faces. The butcher's law in Ipswich, England, warned butchers about spoiled meat:

> All butchers should also take care not to display for sale the meat of diseased animals, or that is rotten or smells bad. Any such meat shall be confiscated on the first occasion; on the second occasion the meat shall be confiscated and its seller sent to the pillory.[9]

Criminals convicted of more serious crimes were punished with bodily disfigurement. Common types included the loss of a thumb, whippings, the gouging of an eye, or the severing of an ear. One fifteenth-century medieval source recommended the branding of thieves:

> Thieves in any man's house in the night, putting him in fear of his life, or breaking up his walls or doors, are burned in the left hand with a hot iron, so that, if they be apprehended again, that mark betrayeth them to have been arraigned of felony before, whereby they are sure at that time to have no mercy.[10]

Feudalism solved some of the problems of the Middle Ages but unintentionally created others. One of the most destructive was a spate of armies, loyal to lords, that uncontrollably roamed the countryside.

Chapter Two

Nobility Fighting Nobility

L ate medieval Europe was a place of violence and anxiety. The feudal system effectively protected Europe from foreign invaders but was utterly ineffective at maintaining internal peace. For much of the eleventh century, local armies on the move, both large and small, were the scourge of Europe. Most of the fighting was the result of feuds between the nobility because they were the ones responsible for financing armies to protect their domains—and interested in extending them whenever possible.

Protection within a fragmented Europe started at the top with kings who needed to defend vaguely defined empires against other kings. In theory, a king could call on all able-bodied men within his kingdom to serve in his army. The same was true of powerful nobles who controlled large provinces as well as lesser nobles looking after small villages. Up and down this loosely structured chain of command, every lord at every level was obligated to

provide soldiers to the lord to whom he owed fealty. Lords could field armies, but they were not always able to control their conduct as they crisscrossed the countryside on their way to battle.

Those who suffered most were the peasants. At any time, an army might appear marching down a dirt road, rowing up a river or Scandinavian fjord, or preparing to lay siege to a castle. The terror that armies inflicted on the surrounding peasant population was immeasurable. Preferred battlefields were often gently rolling plains and meadows, precisely where farmers planted their crops and grazed livestock. Watching from afar, peasant families saw their livelihoods destroyed in an afternoon as their crops were flattened under foot and livestock killed. Mounted knights charging through villages trampled ducks, chickens, goats, and pigs without stopping to compensate the owners. They were also known to steal entire inventories from the shelves of bakers, butchers, and cheese merchants. The rape of women was common.

As the number of battles escalated, lords at all levels became increasingly desperate for more warriors, especially horsemen. Local skirmishes of just a handful of fighters sometimes erupted into larger regional conflicts engulfing dozens of townships and hundreds of combatants.

And on occasion, kings called on their nobles for thousands of armed men.

Lords raising armies, even small ones, faced an expensive proposition. Medieval warriors fought both on foot and on horseback, but centuries of wars had demonstrated the superiority of mounted warriors over foot soldiers. A line of charging cavalry wearing chain-mail armor and

Noblemen on horseback trample slain enemies as they charge into battle. The lord in the foreground is holding up a severed head as a war trophy.

wielding ten-foot-long iron-tipped lances could easily crush opposing foot soldiers. But horses and suits of chain mail were far too costly for the nobility to purchase and provide to their fighters. To solve this problem, those willing to fight and provide their own armor and horse were offered additional land and a higher social status.

Rise of the Knightly Class

Lords with large tracts of land discovered the value of trading plots for the fighting services of mounted warriors from the peasant class. Mounted peasants, in turn, could generate a nice income by renting out their land to farmers and by raising a horse or two of their own for use in battle. As peasants willing to sacrifice their lives in battle volunteered to fight on horseback, they gradually entered the lower echelon of the nobility known as the knights.

As the knights' skills increased, their value to the nobility grew. Foot soldiers stood little chance against an orchestrated cavalry charge of hundreds of mounted and armored knights. Medieval historian Frances Gies conveys the impact of a mounted knight riding down infantry:

> With the lance gripped under his arm and his body secured to his horse by saddle and stirrups, a knight could deliver his blow with the mass and strength of the horse united with his own, creating the sometime overrated but nonetheless effective technique of shock combat.[11]

Knights became indispensable to warfare. Over several generations, their status

as knights became synonymous with the nobility, and conferring knighthood upon a young man became an important ceremony. Sons born to nobility came to bear the title of knight when they reached maturity; noblemen and knights were virtually one and the same, although not all nobles chose to fight.

Local Skirmishes

With the advent of the knightly class, village nobles had the fighting forces necessary to respond to the call to arms of kings or to defend their villages in the more likely event of local skirmishes against neighboring nobles. The historical record speaks of thousands of local skirmishes that plagued medieval Europe because of the greed of the nobility. Village lords gradually acquired a taste for fine foods, silk clothing, and lavish entertainment. Such costly extravagances pressed some lords to look for income beyond their geographic authority. Often, they looked across their village boundaries to neighboring villages to pad their incomes.

Such skirmishes, although constant irritations, were not fought to extend the rule of one village noble over another's but, rather, to tap into valued natural resources. The most valuable natural resources that could be exploited by a neighboring lord were sources of water and transportation. Many eleventh-century records document attempts on the part of village lords to monopolize rivers, streams, roads, and bridges to generate more income. Rivers and streams were necessary not only for drinking water but for powering mills and shipping goods from one town to the

Chain Mail

Warriors learned that they could enhance their odds of surviving vicious sword attacks by covering their bodies with some form of protective armor. The earliest form of body armor was called chain mail—or more simply, mail. Made from thousands of interconnected hard metal rings, mail was woven into a flexible outer metal covering that offered good protection against slicing sword blows.

Most suits of mail, called hauberks, extended from the shoulders to the knees and included the arms. At the center in front and in back it was split from hem to groin to provide the wearer the mobility to run or straddle a horse. Beneath the hauberk, knights wore a quilted or padded jacket called a *gambeson* to prevent chafing and lacerations. The standard hauberk weighed about twenty pounds, but a knight with extra money could purchase a double hauberk that weighed twice as much. To provide similar protection to the head and neck, the knight wore a coif, a chain-mail hood worn over the head and under the helmet that left the face exposed.

The foremost advantage of mail was its defense against bladed weapons; a sword, no matter how sharp, could not easily slash through the metal links. But mail also had disadvantages. If a knight was forced to flee on foot, throwing off the heavy hauberk was incredibly difficult; in fact, knights needed to practice their extrication from it to increase their chances for survival. Also, mail did not make its wearer invulnerable; the force of the blow from a club or mace, a club with a spiked iron ball at one end, could crush the flesh and bones beneath the mail.

next. Likewise, roads and bridges were critical for travelers and merchants. When one village lord, therefore, decided to reroute a stream or charge a tariff to cross a bridge connecting two villages, a windfall profit was to be made.

Unfairly charging tolls to travelers and disrupting commerce were met with threats of war by offended neighboring lords. When negotiations failed to remedy local disputes, it was the obligation of the injured village's noble to make a public call to arms. Once his army was assembled, whether ten men or fifty, the noble led it into the enemy's territory to lay waste to the farmland before his adversary could collect his own army. Setting fire to wheat fields, burning barns, and rustling grazing cattle was often sufficient to destroy the lord's sources of revenue. Other times the invading army rounded up peasant workers and broke their fingers, thereby ensuring that they would be unable to harvest the fall crop. Usually, however, a quick battle resolved the dispute one way or another.

Invading armies often headed straight to a lord's castle and laid siege to it, as was the case reported by an anonymous witness in 1224 when siege machines, archers, and mining crews attacked Bedford castle:

> A stone throwing machine [catapult] attacked the tower every day. . . . In addition, there were very many engines there in which lay hidden both crossbowmen and archers. Furthermore, there was an engine by which under ground diggers called miners undermined the walls of the tower and castle. The castle was taken in four assaults. In the first outer guards were killed. In the second the outer bailey [citadel] was taken where more [guards] were killed. In the third assault, because of the actions of the miners, the walls fell near the old tower and at the fourth assault, a fire was set so that smoke killed many and cracks in the wall appeared.[12]

While sieges trapped the village population inside castle walls, their fields were destroyed and their homes robbed. If the walls of the castle were breached, the lord inside usually made a peace offering to remedy the problems he had caused and to pay damages. Occasionally, however, if conditions were severe, as was the case at Bedford, fighting might kill many and the victor might commandeer the loser's village and all of his vassals. Early village records sometimes reflect

A knight in full armor carries his battle standard as he gallops atop a caparisoned horse.

the change of ownership from one noble family to another.

Greater nobles, those to whom squabbling village nobility owed fealty, often interceded in local disputes and resolved them before violence broke out. Yet if they did not, their position of authority was not altered by the elimination of one of their vassals.

Regional and Family Feuds

A look at a map of mid-eleventh-century Europe partially explains why regional warfare between nobles was rampant. Titled nobility such as dukes, barons, princes, margraves, and counts controlled large provinces that lay within a nation yet were independent of each other.

France, for example, consisted of as many as a dozen provinces such as Toulouse, Normandy, Anjou, Flanders, Ile-de-France, Aquitaine, and Brittany. A traveler in the Holy Roman Empire might pass through more than a dozen provinces journeying north to south, including Friesland, Pomerania, Westphalia, Bavaria, Bohemia, Lotharingia, Thuringia, and several more in northern Italy.

Powerful and aggressive lords often ruled their domains as if they were separate and autonomous kingdoms. They were able to do this, even though they owed allegiance to their kings—and were often related to them—because kings were sometimes weak, far away, and fearful of interfering in the affairs of their lords.

This checkerboard arrangement of autonomous provinces proved to be fertile ground for violent border clashes to conquer neighboring provinces or even eliminate family threats.

Under such circumstances, each lord understood the value of creating alliances with other lords for their mutual protection, especially if they were related. During the reign of King Henry I of France, for example, regional disputes were rampant within the king's family. In 1047 Henry created an alliance with his nephew, William, Duke of Normandy, and together they destroyed a cousin who ruled the region around the city of Caen. A few years after that, however, when William married the daughter of the Count of Flanders and created a family bond with her father,

An invading army lays siege to a castle as villagers and lord seek protection inside.

Henry was wary of William's growing power. Twice during the 1050s, Henry invaded Normandy to destroy William but was forced to retreat on both attempts.

As Henry learned, William could be a truculent adversary. Not satisfied with ruling simply a region of France, William saw an opportunity in 1066 to capture all of England as well. At a time when the English king was vulnerable to attack, William struck.

The Norman Invasion

On occasion, large-scale wars for control of entire nations pitted armies of thousands of warriors against each other. On January 5, 1066, King Edward of England, known as Edward the Confessor, died after a reign of twenty-three years. Because he had not designated an heir to assume the mantle of kingship, his death ignited a rivalry between three claimants to the crown, each of whom was capable of fielding an enormous army. Within months of Edward's death, one of the largest and most significant clashes of medieval armies took place.

Three noblemen living in three different nations made claims to the throne of England. Harold, the only one living in England, asserted his right to the throne as Edward's brother-in-law and court adviser. The day of Edward's burial, the royal council placed the crown on his head and called him king. Across the English Channel, William, Duke of Normandy, also claimed the crown based on kinship with Edward, who was his cousin. The third, Harald Hardrada, the king of Norway, had no family connection but claimed he had a right to the crown based on a verbal agreement.

In mid-September, Hardrada asserted his right to rule England. He landed there with a fleet of 240 ships filled with warriors and advanced to Stamford Bridge just outside of the city of York. When Harold heard of the invasion, he ordered his lords to levy their troops and join him on a forced march from London to York. On September 25, a fierce hand-to-hand battle occurred on the bridge. Finally, the English horsemen stormed across, killing Hardrada and most of his army. Only twenty or so ships of the Norwegian fleet managed to escape and return home.

While Harold was defeating one threat from the north, William was crossing the English Channel from Saint Valery on the east coast of Normandy. He had earlier notified his lords in Normandy, Brittany, and Flanders to gather their armies and come to his assistance. He even went so far as to ask the pope to bless his invasion. As William was landing with his army, Harold hurriedly marched his battle-weary troops south to Hastings, on the English coast south of London. There, on October 14, the two armies clashed.

Harold positioned his seven-thousand-man army opposite the ten to twelve thousand men of William's force. Roughly one-quarter of each army consisted of mounted knights, with the remainder equally divided between foot soldiers and archers. The two armies were the biggest array of soldiers on a single battlefield that either country had seen. The battle was witnessed by the Norman historian Orderic Vitalis, who recorded this account:

The Bayeux Tapestry

Immediately following the Battle of Hastings in 1066, one of the most unusual historical records ever conceived was created in the French city of Bayeux, on the Normandy peninsula. The Bayeux Tapestry is an account of the battle depicted in linen threads.

This hand-stitched tapestry, which today still resides in Bayeux, is 231 feet long and 20 inches wide. It depicts the major figures of the battle by name. It also features scenes of combat, battlefield strategies and army positioning, and a wealth of stitched illustrations of mounted knights, their armor, and castle architecture of the time.

Of all the tapestry's illustrations, those of knights' armor and weapons are among the most intriguing. Historians have concluded from many segments that most knights at that time rode into battle with only chain mail and a helmet to protect themselves. Those with chain mail are covered from neck to knee, and the helmets are slightly conical in shape and lack faceplates. None of the horses are shown in armor although some are caparisoned, draped neck to tail with colorful low-hanging blankets.

The tapestry depicts a wide variety of weaponry. Almost all mounted knights carry a shield, always in the left hand, and a lance in the right hand. Some knights carry lances with small pennants bearing their coat of arms attached. Those without shield and lance are shown with wooden clubs, and a few carry a mace, a wooden club with an iron knob on the end.

The sound of the trumpets in both armies was the terrible signal for beginning the battle. The Normans made the first attack with ardor and gallantry, spreading wounds and death through the ranks of the English by showers of arrows and bolts. The battle raged for some time with the utmost violence between both parties. . . . In this manner the Normans suddenly wheeling their horses, cut their pursuers off from the main body, surrounded and slew them. When thousands were thus slaughtered, the Normans attacked the survivors with still greater vigor.[13]

Knights and infantry fought until the late afternoon, when William ordered his men to charge the English center. As they rushed forward, breaking through the English line, Harold was apparently knocked from his horse by an arrow that pierced his eye, killing him.

The English army suffered terrible losses and surrendered. William took charge of England and marched to London, where he was crowned William the Conqueror, king of England, at the abbey church of Westminster. Thus began the Norman occupation of England, Wales, Scotland, and later Ireland.

Nobility Out of Control

Not all violence was expressed on the battlefield. Many knights, struggling to make enough money to cover their expenses, succumbed to reckless abuse of their fighting prowess. Most owed their lords forty days a year fighting in the army as part of their feudal contract but were free to do other things the remainder of the year. To supplement their incomes, many knights chose to use their fighting skills in ways unrelated to their feudal contracts. The most common way was to fight as mercenaries, or soldiers hired for pay. A few accepted pay to fight in trials by combat, while others turned to the age-old profession of robbery.

Nobles capable of arming themselves and in need of money crisscrossed the roads of Europe as mercenaries in search of a fight. According to historian Maurice Keen:

The Norman cavalry advances in this scene from the Bayeux Tapestry. The tapestry was created to commemorate the Norman victory at the Battle of Hastings in 1066.

There were sovereign princes at one another's throat everywhere: this indeed is one of the distinctive features of the period. One party to a quarrel could hardly abstain from employing mercenaries unless it could trust the adversary to do so too, which it clearly could not.[14]

Local and regional wars were common enough to provide employment a few days' ride from home. Knights camped at the intersections of major roads to gather information about skirmishes from travelers. Once a battle was found, mercenaries offered their services to the lord paying the highest wage. Mercenaries were not highly respected by other nobility because their allegiances in battle were not determined by friendship, fealty, or morality. Yet they flourished, sometimes fighting for just one day but other times for months. Welsh historian Dave Etheridge believes that mercenaries expanded the scope of war: "It is clear that the availability of mercenaries in the eleventh century promoted warfare on a greater scale than was usual before."[15]

Occasionally knights accepted jobs representing other persons who were involved in disputes that could be reconciled only by what was called a judicial combat. These combats emerged out of a shortage of law courts and law codes for resolving disputes. Many European countries support-

This medieval tapestry depicts mercenaries in close combat. As war was a fact of life in the Late Middle Ages, these soldiers for hire easily found employment.

ed the use of judicial combat, one man fighting another, to determine a person's guilt or innocence. The loser of the fight was obligated to compensate the winner in some way. Oftentimes, litigants unwilling or incapable of engaging in these combats were permitted to employ knights to fight in their place. This was not considered merely a business arrangement. Medieval minds saw it quite differently. To them, knights were acting as the hand of God to reveal the innocent and the guilty persons.

When knights were down on their luck and legitimate forms of combat were not available, a few turned to thievery. Europe during the Middle Ages developed a vast network of roads that carried thousands of foot and mounted travelers from Rome as far north as Amsterdam and Copenhagen. Unfortunately for unarmed, weary travelers, especially wealthy nobility, brigand knights might descend upon them, blocking their route until money was handed over. Medieval travelers wrote about knights who rode down from their castles to rob travelers on the roads or shut them up in their castles to be held for ransom. One self-confessed brigand knight explained to his band of reluctant men that robbery would make them rich: "It will be a happy day. For we shall seize the usurers' [moneylenders'] goods, and pack animals will no longer pass safely, or the mayor journey without fear, or the merchant on his way to France, but the man full of courage will be rich."[16]

Fighting nobility created unprecedented chaos throughout Europe. Everyone saw the need to reduce levels of bloodshed, but without a powerful central government, no king dared to act. The only authority able to exercise control over the nobility, the Catholic Church, recognized the need. According to historian Frank E. Smitha, it was common to find "wars by ego-driven young nobles on horseback—Christian noble against Christian noble. The Church was eager to limit their fighting."[17]

Controlling Reckless Nobility

One church leader, the archbishop of Bordeaux, seized the opportunity to curb reckless violence. He issued an edict called the Peace of God that was intended to rein in rowdy warriors by obligating them to the church. His edict threatened to expel from the church any knight who raided churches, attacked unarmed clergy and peasants, or robbed anyone traveling to or from church. Other archbishops throughout Europe supported the Peace of God, and the general level of violence against the clergy and poor declined.

The Peace of God, however, required strengthening. A second edict called the Truce of God ordered knights to suspend fighting between Thursday and Sunday

The Knighting Ceremony

Initially the knighting ceremony was little more than an open-handed, bone-jarring blow to the neck of a young warrior followed by an admonition to conduct himself with bravery and honor. By the eleventh century, however, the ceremony became more elaborate, symbolizing the investiture of authority, the attainment of a young nobleman's manhood, and his entrance into the warrior class of the social elite.

The full ceremony lasted several days and was filled with symbolic meaning. It began at the church with a nightlong prayer vigil. During the vigil the young man's weapons were placed on the altar, symbolizing the role of the church in his life. This was followed by a sunrise bath for the young warrior that represented the washing away of youthful indiscretion so that he was prepared for the seriousness of battle. After the bath, he dressed in a simple white linen tunic symbolizing purity, a scarlet mantle for nobility, and black shoes denoting his eventual death. A priest then said mass for him before a gathering of royal friends and family.

Kneeling before his lord, the squire repeated a brief oath promising to fight for and protect the general welfare, and solemnly bowed his head. At that moment, the lord stepped forward, drew his own sword, and held it high above the young man's head. He then called out the squire's name and conferred knighthood by placing the flat side of his sword blade on one shoulder and then the other. These two symbolic blows marked the moment the squire became a knight.

and on all saints' and holy days. It also required knights to allow merchants and travelers to pass safely and to assist the poor and those in ill health. The combined result of these two edicts not only reduced needless bloodshed (although far from all of it) but obligated knights to protect those in need of assistance.

Contained within these two edicts were the seeds of chivalry, a code of behavior that gradually attempted—though not always successfully—to control knights' bellicose behavior toward each other and others. It was the opinion of church leaders that in addition to fighting for the nobility, knights had the ethical and moral obligation to come to the assistance of unarmed citizens in need of aid. Chivalry was based on courtesy and honor toward the church as well as the innocent and defenseless poor. The twelfth-century philosopher John of Salisbury posed the question, "What is the function of orderly knighthood?" His answer, which reflected a knight's chivalric obligations, was respected and repeated by many knights who revered him:

A young squire kneels as his lord confers knighthood upon him and a church official offers his blessing.

> To defend the Church, to assail infidelity, to venerate the priesthood, to protect the poor from injuries, to pacify the province, to pour out their blood for their brothers, and, if need be, to lay down their lives. The high praises of God are in their throat, and two-edged swords are in their hands to execute punishment on the nations and rebuke upon the peoples, and to bind their kings and their nobles in link of iron.[18]

Placing moral and behavioral restraints on the nobility bestowed a religious obligation on medieval warriors. Not only were knights duty bound to their lords as part of the feudal system, they also became duty bound to fight in the service of God if the pope should issue the command.

Chapter Three

The Crusades and Their Contribution to Europe

At the close of the eleventh century, the papal command for a holy war was issued. For the first time ever, the influence of the medieval church reached beyond the pulpit to all of Europe as its citizens were asked to prepare for a holy war called a Crusade. Before this time popes had given their blessings to kings going off to battle against a rival king, and on occasion they even raised their own armies. But at the end of the eleventh century, the pope perceived a threat to all of Christendom that he believed required the combined armies of Europe.

Of all the wars waged during the Late Middle Ages, none had a more profound impact on European society and culture than the Crusades. What began as a holy war to recapture Christian lands from the Muslims in the eastern Mediterranean (and ended nearly two hundred years later in failure) proved to be the event that shaped Europe more than any other. In the opinion of medieval historian Frances

Gies, the Crusades were "the largest single event in the annals of the Middle Ages."[19]

The Crusades began when Muslim armies occupying the Holy Land harassed European Christians making religiously motivated trips, or pilgrimages, there. Pilgrimages were visits to the cities and shrines associated with Jesus. Christians believed that these exhausting and difficult journeys were a demonstration of penance for sins they may have committed and would bring God's forgiveness.

Pilgrimages to Jerusalem

For centuries, thousands of Europeans annually embarked on lengthy pilgrimages lasting several months to visit and pay homage to religious sites in the Holy Land. Favorite destinations were Jerusalem, Bethlehem, the Sea of Galilee, and dozens of other biblical sites associated with Jesus. While there, pilgrims sought out prayer shrines containing ven-

The Road to Jerusalem: The Routes and Events of the First Crusade

Pope Urban II addresses the church council and calls for the first crusade in 1095.

In 1099 crusaders attack the city of Jerusalem.

ENGLAND

GERMANY

North Atlantic Ocean

Bruges

Bouillon

Vezelay

Regensburg

HUNGARY

FRANCE

Clermont

Toulouse

Marseille

Venice

Pisa

ITALY

Rome

Naples

Brindisi

Bari

SICILY

Zara

Durazzo

BULGARIA

Black Sea

Constantinople
Bosporus

Nicaea

Dorylaeum

SPAIN

Mediterranean Sea

CRETE

CYPRUS

Edessa

Antioch

Tripoli

Tyre

Acre

Jerusalem

N
W   E
S

➤➤➤ Routes of the First Crusade

erated Christian relics such as pieces of the cross on which Jesus was crucified, the nails pounded through his hands, the crown of thorns he wore before his death, and an assortment of other sacred artifacts, some perhaps authentic but most not. Pilgrims believed these relics possessed curative powers. Visiting and praying before them was thought to cure sickness, increase one's chances for entering heaven, and even release a dead relative's soul from hell.

In the middle of the eleventh century, hundreds of years of safe passage came to an end. The Muslims, who lived in the Holy Land, found the pilgrimages to be an affront to their religion. Over time, an animosity grew between Christians and Muslims and eventually Muslim soldiers began blocking the route to the Holy Land. Christians continued to make pilgrimages, however, so the Muslim soldiers began killing them. Vowing to keep the routes open and the sites and relics well protected, the pope threatened a war intended to rid the Holy Land of Muslims.

The Papal Call to Arms

The call to crusade against the Muslims went out in 1095. Pope

Pilgrims travel to the Holy Land by boat. The refusal of Muslims to allow safe passage to pilgrims sparked the First Crusade in the late eleventh century.

Urban II addressed a church council in the French city of Clermont before cardinals and bishops and the French nobility. Urban called for a full-scale crusade of armies representing all European nations to march to the Holy Land and drive out the Muslims. Urban emphasized the importance of the Crusades and drove emotions to a frenzy, saying:

> It is the imminent peril threatening you and all the faithful which has brought us here. From the confines of Jerusalem a horrible tale has gone forth . . . an accursed race, a race utterly alienated from God . . . has invaded the lands of Christians and has depopulated them by sword, pillage, and fire. On whom therefore, is the labor of avenging these wrongs and of recovering these territories incumbent, if not upon you? Enter upon the road to the Holy Sepulcher [Jesus' tomb]; wrest that land from the wicked race, and subject it to yourselves.[20]

Urban's dramatic call to arms electrified the crowd. When he completed his exhortion for war, the crowd began chanting *"Deus volt, Deus volt, Deus volt,"* meaning "God wills it."

After three years of planning and organizing, kings from many nations finally raised armies that now gathered for the march east. As each mounted knight and foot soldier set out for his long journey, he

Addressing the church council in the French city of Clermont, Pope Urban II calls for a crusade against the Muslims in the Holy Land.

swore an oath to remain faithful to Christianity and to abide by the code of chivalry. With that oath, each then tore up bits of clothing into strips and sewed them on his shield and cloak in the form of the cross. Fulcher of Chartres, a historian who witnessed this act, proclaimed, "O how fitting it was, how pleasing to us all to see these crosses."[21]

For the first time in European history, all European nations were unified against a common enemy. Putting aside most of their local bickering in the face of an alien threat, soldiers speaking different languages and representing different traditions united for a common cause. As the crusaders set out, they could not know that

On the Road to Jerusalem

The road to Jerusalem was not the same for all pilgrims. The nobility traveled in the comfort of horse-drawn carriages and stopped at inns for the night where hot meals of meats, vegetables, breads, desserts, and wine energized them for the next day's travel. Under these ideal conditions, travelers arrived in Jerusalem within one month, depending on their city of departure. Poor pilgrims, on the other hand, walked to Jerusalem, slept along the road, and begged for food during their three-month journey.

The value of the pilgrimage for the most devout pilgrims was the suffering experienced en route. These pilgrims, although a minority, believed that by suffering along the way they were demonstrating to God the sincerity of their religious commitment. Some took the pilgrimage so seriously that they wore the coarsest clothing so that it scratched and chafed their skin. Some even traveled the entire journey barefoot, carrying a staff to assist them when they became lame. The more they suffered, they believed, the greater the likelihood that God would look favorably upon their lives.

While pilgrims suffered, entrepreneurs profited. An industry grew up along land and sea routes in which shop owners, hoteliers, tavern owners, and ship captains profited. There were also sellers of souvenirs and pilgrim's badges. Pilgrims who chose not to complete the trip to Jerusalem bought badges and artifacts to take home that created the false impression that they had gone all the way. Some even returned home having purchased worthless pieces of paper granting them pardons and forgiveness for their sins and assurances of a place in heaven.

---

their Crusade would be but the first of nine that collectively would last almost two hundred years and would fail in their objective.

Suffering and Horrid Warfare

The First Crusade generally set the tone for the rest. Although the pope portrayed the Crusade as a holy war, knights and foot soldiers saw it differently. Many of them, struggling to earn a meager living under the manorial system, viewed the war as an opportunity to make money. In addition to venerated Christian relics, the Holy Land was also known to be rich in gold, silver, and precious jewels. Greed, more than spiritual conviction, fired the soldiers' imaginations.

In 1098 four thousand mounted knights, ten thousand infantry, and fourteen thousand archers from across Europe joined the initial campaign now known to historians as the First Crusade. The lure of riches faded quickly as the army made its long trek. They marched from France, Germany, and England through northern Italy, then across Eastern Europe, and finally through

Turkey. They covered hundreds of miles through scorching deserts and deep snow in the mountain passes. The crusaders ran out of fresh water on numerous occasions, and according to survivor Peter the Hermit, some were reduced to drinking their own urine, animal blood, and water drawn from sewage ditches:

> Our people were in such distress from thirst that they bled their horses and asses and drank the blood; others let their handkerchiefs down into the cistern and squeezed out the water from them into their mouths; some urinated into one another's hollowed hands and drank; and others dug up the moist ground and lay down on their backs and spread the earth over their breasts to relieve the excessive dryness of thirst.[22]

Food was another problem. Most food was purchased from local people along the

An illustration from a medieval manuscript shows a crusader cutting the head off a fellow knight in order to seize his booty during the First Crusade.

route at exorbitant prices until money ran low. Then the soldiers had to forage and scrounge for whatever they could find or steal. Christian historians accompanying the crusaders hoping to write of their glorious acts of Christian chivalry instead reported desperate acts of pillaging and plundering from peasants' farms. Hardships along the route caused many to abandon the Crusade and shamefully creep back home.

In late 1098 roughly ten thousand of the initial twenty-eight thousand crusaders gathered at their ultimate objective,

Eight crusaders loot a church in the Holy Land of all its valuables.

Jerusalem. The attack commenced in the summer of 1099. The entire city was protected by high walls and stout gates that crusaders eventually scaled. What then took place was a horrid spectacle. Fulcher of Chartres wrote a lengthy account of the killing of an estimated seventy thousand Muslims at the Temple of Solomon:

A great fight took place in the court and porch of the temple, where they were unable to escape from our gladiators. Many fled to the roof of the temple of Solomon, and were shot with arrows, so that they fell to the ground dead. In this temple almost ten thousand were killed. Indeed, if you had been there you would have seen our feet colored to our ankles with the blood of the slain. But what more shall I relate? None of them were left alive; neither women nor children were spared.[23]

Initially, during this first of nine Crusades, the European forces won decisive victories only to lose them on subsequent smaller and less dramatic Crusades. In the end, after almost two hundred years of sporadic fighting, what was won early on was lost, leaving the Holy Land in the hands of the enemy.

The Shame of Pillaging

The destruction of entire cities and their populations was just one of the shameful acts attributed to crusaders. Another was tied directly to the crude and unsophisticated eco-

Crusaders storm the walls of Jerusalem and butcher the city's Muslim inhabitants in 1099. Less than one hundred years later, the Muslims recaptured Jerusalem.

nomics of manorialism. The financial obligations for supporting the crusaders fell to Europe's nobility, and the costs were staggering. Paying for a soldier's food, equipment, and incidental expenses was a hefty obligation. During the first Crusades, warriors were obligated to serve forty days without pay, during which time they either carried their own food or purchased it with their own money. After that period, most agreed to accept the spoils of war as compensation. It was customary to allow the fighting men to claim the lion's share of the spoils of war, including money, gold, jewelry, and other objects of value that were taken from the homes of the wealthy, mosques, and commercial centers.

Far from home after the first forty-day period, crusaders found that spoils of war were not as easily gotten as new recruits were led to believe. Desperate to keep the troops on the march, leaders gave their men permission to pillage farms and villages in exchange for the promised wages and spoils that were not forthcoming.

Stories of poor peasants helplessly watching the looting of their livestock and grain bins foreshadowed their starvation with the arrival of winter. Those few peasants

The Hanseatic League

In the twelfth century, an alliance of one hundred mostly German cities vested in trade formed a monopolistic trading partnership called the Hanseatic League. The league's name derived from the medieval German term *Hanse*, which meant group or company.

The Hanseatic League initially formed for self-protection because there was no German national government capable of providing the military power needed to ensure trade security. Once they established security by deploying their own warships, the Hanseatic towns became powerful and wealthy enough to negotiate exclusive trading rights and, wherever possible, trade monopolies. In this regard, the league solved the problem of sending out trading ships without the support of a strong central government obligated to protect them.

Without a central government supporting them yet with the power of the league, its merchants were able to convince the kings of England and Denmark to grant them special trading privileges such as reduced import taxes and access to markets not available to other trading cities. So independent and powerful was the Hanseatic League that it hired soldiers to fight wars to preserve its monopoly over trade routes and trading cities until its demise in the Late Middle Ages. At that time, competition from powerful Dutch and English traders conspired to destroy the league.

who did resist, often with little more than shovels and pitchforks, were ruthlessly killed and their homes raided. Pillaging crusaders cut a swath of destruction ten miles wide as they marched to feed their armies of hungry men. Only foods that peasants hid in haystacks or barns was left untouched. Pigs, cattle, chickens, and geese were slaughtered and eaten, often raw, on the spot.

Pillaging was a violation of the code of chivalry and was considered morally reprehensible. Nonetheless, pillaging poor villagers was the only option that remained for hungry crusaders. Kings and their lords were willing to turn a blind eye to the obvious violations of the code of chivalry that forbade inflicting injury on poor and innocent civilians. This irresponsible policy caused kings and lords to lose all control of their men.

While most crusaders struggled to survive the wars, a few focused their attention on the exotic goods available from Muslim merchants. Many crusaders who embarked as warriors returned home as international traders.

The Emergence of International Trade

Crusaders marching through dozens of thriving port cities and inland towns were exposed to exotic merchandise they had never seen back home in Europe. Attracted to the new smells, tastes, and sights of Middle Eastern goods, a few traders and other businessmen recognized the potential for commercial success. At the conclusion of the Crusades, the region most changed by the events of the wars was Europe, not the Holy Land. Christian crusaders lost the military war against the Muslims, but Christian traders won many lucrative commercial opportunities. Some crusading armies that initially set out to liberate the Holy Land from the Muslims returned home to sell at great profit the goods they had acquired there. The ships owned by wealthy merchants that carried crusading soldiers to the war returned home loaded with enough exotic commodities to propel their owners into the ranks of the new merchant class of millionaires.

Some of the nobles who had led armies to the Holy Land became familiar with the alien culture of the eastern Mediterranean and saw an opportunity for financial profit.

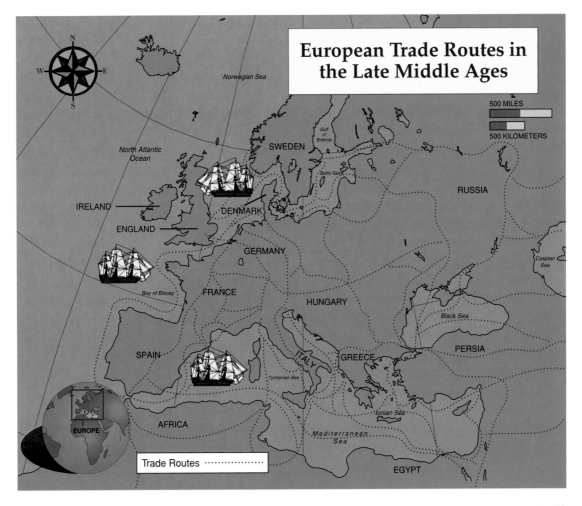

European Trade Routes in the Late Middle Ages

500 MILES

500 KILOMETERS

Norwegian Sea

North Atlantic Ocean

Gulf of Bothnia

SWEDEN

Baltic Sea

RUSSIA

IRELAND

DENMARK

ENGLAND

GERMANY

Caspian Sea

Bay of Biscay

FRANCE

HUNGARY

Black Sea

SPAIN

ITALY

GREECE

PERSIA

Tyrrhenian Sea

EUROPE

AFRICA

Ionian Sea

Mediterranean Sea

Trade Routes ·············

EGYPT

They organized trading partnerships and loaded seagoing freighters bound for the Holy Land with cloth, armor, silver, salted fish, and leather in exchange for a long list of expensive goods demanded by lords and ladies in Europe. Freighters returned with their hulls loaded with exotic foods such as dates, salted squid, honey-soaked desserts, and ostrich eggs. They also carried exotic spices, so expensive that some were sold by the individual seed, including pepper, cloves, cardamom, ginger, saffron, and cinnamon. Stylish women looked forward to crates filled with jewelry made of ivory, pearls, and malachite, and elegant gowns of colorful silks, brocades, satins, and feathers.

Well-to-do crusaders who preferred to spend their time trading rather than fighting made fortunes. As their wealth grew, some put their money to work by loaning it to other men interested in establishing businesses in major cities or to kings in need of more money to hire mercenaries for future Crusades. Bankers made a fortune in 1145 when the French king Louis VII put out the call for the Second Crusade and borrowed money to pay for it. The arrangement worked out so well that all of the succeeding Crusades were funded in part by loans from burgeoning banking houses, most of which were in northern Italian trading cities such as Venice, Florence, and Pisa. According to historian Scott J. Beem, feudal lords "provided shipping and even built their own fleets and developed and harnessed an advanced array of banking institutions, and provided advice and guidance to kings and upper nobility."[24]

Newfound Wealth

As trade flourished, so did cities with access to the Mediterranean Sea. Far from the small plots of land tilled by penniless farmers, commercial centers prospered. The cities that initially benefited from trade with the eastern Mediterranean were seaports in northern Italy, followed by those in southern France, Spain, and eventually the Netherlands, Denmark, and Germany. In dozens of coastal cities, shipbuilders, ship owners, traders, and bankers began amassing unprecedented fortunes.

Money, and lots of it, set merchants apart from the rest of feudal society. Cosmopolitan entrepreneurs defied the three traditional classes that defined medieval society and recognized no feudal obligations to the nobility. They became the merchant class. They had enough money to live more luxuriously than most nobility and to hire their own private bands of bodyguards.

As their bank accounts swelled, merchants pioneered the lending of money at high interest rates, allowing them to make money not only at their professions but also on their surplus money. The banking and lending industries became so profitable in Florence that in 1252 the city minted its own gold coin called the florin, which became the standard currency for all of Europe for hundreds of years. Powerful banking and shipping families became famous for their considerable fortunes and richly decorated palatial estates.

The emergence of wealthy families created generations of descendants who no longer faced the grim reality of tilling the soil behind a plow horse or working in cities at menial

This woodcut illustrates the size of the medieval city of Verona, Italy. In the wake of the Crusades, large cities began to spring up all over Europe.

The Significance of the Spice Trade

Before the Crusades, the Muslims kept Europe in the dark regarding the source of many rare and desirable spices such as pepper, cinnamon, cloves, nutmeg, and ginger. They bought their spices from Indian traders who had obtained them from Chinese and Javanese merchants. But because of the value of spices, worth more per pound than any food and more than many rare gems, Arabs refused to tell Christians visiting the Holy Land where they came from.

Contrary to widespread beliefs, spices were not used to improve rotting meats because when meats decay, they become poisonous and no amount of spices can reverse putrefaction. Spices then, as now, were used to enhance the pleasurable taste of foods.

Because of the high cost of spices, only the wealthy could enjoy them. During the Late Middle Ages in Europe, a pound of ginger was the same price as a sheep; a pound of mace could buy three sheep or half a cow; and cloves cost the equivalent of about twenty dollars a pound. Pepper, always the greatest prize, was counted out peppercorn by peppercorn. The guards on London docks had to have their pockets sewn shut to prevent them from stealing any spices. In the eleventh century, many towns kept their accounts in pepper; taxes and rents were assessed and paid in this spice, and a sack of it was worth a man's life. Spices were even used as ransom for captured noblemen; one of the more well-known spice ransoms was three hundred pounds of pepper.

jobs for subsistence wages. For the first time since the decline of big cities following the collapse of the Roman Empire, the children of wealthy non-noble parents had leisure time to pursue their own interests.

The Rise of Cosmopolitan Cities

One of the most important results of the Crusades and the trade that they spawned was the rise of cosmopolitan cities that grew in wealth, size, and sophistication. Commerce never ceased before the Crusades nor did most cities disappear, but prior to the Crusades, Europe was princi-

pally agrarian and its most important political and cultural centers were fortified castles, not cities. Following the Crusades, however, a handful of cities prospered and developed great universities, cathedrals, trading markets, and seats of government. Although the urban population of Europe rarely exceeded 10 percent, it was disproportionately wealthy, educated, and influential. The Muslim writer Ibn Hawqal, who reported the wealth of several Italian trading centers, commented on the coastal town of Amalfi: "It is the most prosperous town in Lombardy, the most noble, the most illustrious on account of its conditions, the most affluent and splendid." In a visit to Venice, Hawqal highlighted its commercial wealth by noting, "Venice is a nation that does not plough, sow, or gather vintage [grapes]."[25]

As cities grew more cosmopolitan, they attracted more people. Although small by modern standards, Paris had nearly 100,000 people at its height at the end of the Crusades. The large cities of Italy, such as Genoa, Florence, and Venice, had about twenty-five thousand people each; in German cities, however, populations rarely exceeded ten thousand. One traveling writer described with amazement Milan as having

> 120 lawyers, 1,500 notaries, 28 expert physicians, 150 surgeons, eight grammar teachers, over seventy teachers of reading, and book scribers [copyists] number forty. The ovens in the city cooking bread for the citizens are 200, wine-merchants selling wonderful wines of all sorts are without doubt over one thousand, and butchers over 440.[26]

Few cosmopolitan cities were planned. Almost all had at least three centers: the marketplace, the major cathedral, and the castle. Because these were the most important locations, simple homes tended to congregate around them. Few streets were paved; most were dark, narrow, and dirty. Most people lived on the top floor of two-story buildings, while taverns selling food, inns providing lodging, or retail shops selling a variety of goods were located on the ground floor. Buildings were crowded together because most major cities were ringed by stone walls for defense, and everyone tried to fit inside. Periodically the population grew too large and new walls had to be built.

Merchants in cosmopolitan trading cities in close proximity, such as those clustered around northern Italy, western Netherlands, northern Germany, and southern Denmark, were reluctant to accept any sort of imperial authority that would cost them money. Instead, they established trading leagues to oppose excessive taxation imposed by kings and princes and to monopolize trade for their own benefit. Following occasional open warfare with noble families, leagues won concessions from them, and functioned without much interference.

The Crusades may have been a boon for warriors and businessmen, but not everyone was interested in those two professions. Some, especially those within the church, viewed soldiers and merchants as predatory, immoral men. For those who shared such moralistic views, monasteries offered a more pious and culturally productive life.

Chapter Four

Contributions of Pious Brethren

In the midst of the pall of war, one alternative for men with an interest in a life detached from the brutish work of fighting and tilling fields was to join the company of pious brethren. During the beginning of the Late Middle Ages, increasing numbers of men saw value in joining a monastery and living secluded from family and village life. Their individual decisions had a profound collective impact that enormously enriched European culture.

The growing interest in joining monasteries was a response to the desire to return to the fundamental teachings of Christ: reject war, avoid the temptations of the material world, show compassion for the weak, find comfort in prayer, and enrich the mind. Monks believed that emulating Christ's teachings could be achieved only by being sequestered from conventional life found in towns and villages. To that end, tens of thousands of men flocked to walled monasteries that were closed to all except monks willing to take vows to live alone, silently, and in prayer.

Monasteries provided a basic social structure for monks while they worked and prayed isolated from the rest of the world. Monks were a part of the Catholic Church yet far removed from it. Unlike village priests who interacted with villagers daily and ministered to their spiritual needs, monks sequestered themselves in remote locations and rarely went outside monastery walls. Within the walls, monks committed themselves to performing *Opus Dei*, Latin for the "work of God." It was their variety of *Opus Dei* that contributed immeasurably to European culture. They established the great traditions of caring for the poor and the sick, creating orphanages, engaging in scholarly pursuits, obtaining university educations, and preserving books written by revered Greek and Roman thinkers.

A monk leads a child into a monastery as his parents say goodbye.

St. Francis of Assisi

One of the most renowned pious brethren was St. Francis of Assisi. Born in Assisi, Italy, in 1182, Francis was the son of a wealthy cloth merchant. He lived his early years recklessly until a grave illness and then fighting in the Crusades nearly cost him his life.

One day, in the Church of San Damiano, while reflecting on his life, he believed he heard Christ telling him to join a monastery and perform *Opus Dei*. Despite his father's disapproval, Francis took the vows of poverty and renounced his father's wealth. His father was outraged, and during a public confrontation, Francis handed his father all of his money, took off his expensive clothes, and walked away naked to the monastery.

Francis committed himself to serving the poor and helping lepers, who were shunned by society because the disease that covered their bodies with sores was falsely believed to be easily contagious. Francis cared for them, fed them, and bathed their sores. He gained further fame by carrying stones lying useless in fields and using them to repair the Church of San Damiano. He received his meals not by asking for money but by scrounging crusts and discarded vegetables, and by working as a laborer paid in food rather than in money.

Francis soon attracted followers. He preached the necessity of a poor, simple life based on the ideals taught by Jesus. Pope Innocent III, who admired his way of life, gave him and his disciples permission to give sermons on many topics and ordained Francis a deacon in the church. Francis died on October 3, 1226.

The interest in monastic life ebbed and flowed over time, but at the outset of the Late Middle Ages it was particularly strong. Many men such as St. Francis of Assisi led the movement to join any of two thousand monasteries throughout Europe in response to Christ's teachings and the rejection of blatant and shameful corruption within the church.

Church Corruption

During the eleventh century, the authority of the church declined when it lost control over the practice of appointing men to the highest church offices. Feudal lords controlled most of the land and because of their wealth and political authority, many believed it was their right to appoint new bishops and abbots rather than allowing the pope to make the appointments. Many lords made a public spectacle of appointing new bishops and abbots by holding a ceremony called an investiture, during which the lord handed the new man two symbols of church authority, a ring and an elaborately carved staff. By placing the ring on the new bishop's finger, the lord was symbolically expressing his authority over him.

The increasing practice of secular investiture worsened when the nobility realized they could sell high church offices, a corrupt practice called simony. For a large sum of money, a nobleman could sell a church office to a friend, relative, or another noble in exchange for some other favor. Nobles even sold them to ambitious priests who hoped to climb higher within the bureaucracy of the church. A newly selected bishop or abbot owed the noble who invested him a large sum. To raise the money, the bishop or abbot took it from the Sunday collection plate or demanded

St. Francis of Assisi, seen here in an Italian fresco, dedicated his life to serving the poor and the sick.

fees from his priests as a way of expressing their allegiance to him. In either case, money rather than merit was at the root of church appointments.

Many clergymen who bought offices from the nobility in turn sold them to others within the church. The pathetic state of affairs into which the church sank was reflected in letters written by many bishops. One boasted, "I gave gold and received the episcopate. I ordain a priest and I receive gold; I make a deacon and I receive a heap of silver. Behold the gold which I gave I have once more replaced in my purse."[27] As the purses of bishops and abbots filled with coins, they became increasingly uninterested in performing their duties. Many stopped caring for the poor, attending burial services, or baptizing babies.

Corruption even found its way to the office of the pope, as medieval historian Anne Fremantle explains:

> The papacy itself suffered deep degradation. It was bought and sold among a group of Roman noble families, and at one point there were three men who claimed the office as of family right. The murder or poisoning of a pope of a rival faction was not uncommon.[28]

For many years the average term of a pope was merely three years. Some of the popes were embarrassments to the office. Several had reputations for castrating men they despised, openly carrying on affairs with women, fathering children, and appearing in public drunk.

Corruption within the church hierarchy became so rampant and public that many priests voiced complaints. Some even quit in disgust. Others distanced themselves from the Vatican by joining monasteries in remote villages, in desert communities, and even on mountaintops.

Monasteries of Pious Brethren

Monks living in remote monasteries learned to accept and value solitary, simple, and celibate lives. Such reclusions were not new. They were rooted in dozens of biblical stories describing the lives of St. Mark, John the Baptist, and Jesus, each of whom isolated himself from society for long periods of time in order to achieve a higher level of spirituality. Ascetic lives included self-denial: the rejection of normal pleasures such as comfortable clothes, warm meals, casual conversations, and soft beds. The saying most often quoted by monks to explain their pursuit of self-denial was Jesus's comment, "If you would be perfect, go, sell what you possess and give to the poor, and you will have treasure in heaven; and come, follow me."[29]

The charter of monasteries was to operate completely free of lay control and distant from parish churches. Many simple parish priests tried to practice various forms of social and personal asceticism but none as austere as monks. St. Jerome, one of the early monks, made this distinction between the lives of monks and village priests:

> If you wish to perform the office of a priest, then live in cities and townships,

Monks typically lived in self-sufficient monasteries, where they raised their own food. Here, monks harvest wheat in the fields.

and make the salvation of others the gain of your soul. But if you desire to be called a monk, which is solitary, what are you doing in cities, which are after all the dwelling places not of solitaries, but of the many?[30]

Without the distractions of village life, monks focused their time on a variety of daily tasks. Monasteries offered monks a range of choices for their *Opus Dei*. Prayer, solemn contemplation, and labor in the fields raising food were required of all brethren, but a few hours each day were left to their discretion. During the Late Middle Ages, one of the *Opus Dei* preferred by many monks, which set them apart from the rest of medieval society, was education.

Contributions of Pious Brethren ■ 59

Master Illustrators

Master illustrators captured the attention of wealthy patrons of the arts and manuscripts. The most renowned illustrators, the three Limburg brothers, found fame illuminating a book titled *Les très riches heures*, French for "The Very Rich Hours." This medieval prayer book, used for private devotion, contained prayers and meditations appropriate to certain hours of the day, days of the week, months, or seasons. It is considered by most art historians to be the finest example of all surviving illuminated manuscripts because of the colors and artistic quality. Today it remains one of the greatest art treasures of France.

The pictures in this edition of *Les très riches heures* were painted by the Limburg brothers for the wealthy Frenchman Jean Duc de Berry. Each illuminated page depicts details of medieval activities such as nobles hunting and attending elaborate dinner parties, peasants tilling the soil, woodsmen chopping logs, and squires saddling horses. All depictions were painted in vivid blues, reds, yellows, and mixes of other colors derived from crushing a variety of minerals, plants, insects, chemicals, and shellfish. Art historians consider each page to be a priceless masterpiece.

Pictured here is a vividly illustrated page from the prayer book, Les très riches heures.

Preserving Ancient Writings

Monks established a robust interest in and tradition for learning. One of their earliest academic interests was copying ancient manuscripts, one of the most valued *Opus Dei* they performed. Long before the invention of the printing press, the only way to copy an existing book was to do so by hand, a process that could take many months depending on the book's length and language. By the Late Middle Ages, thousands of old Greek and Roman manuscripts had already been lost because the material they were written on—papyrus, a form of paper made from plant fibers, and parchment, which is the dried and treated skins of goats and sheep—had cracked and disintegrated. As the most literate segment of medieval society, many monks adopted the view that they could best serve the church by "fighting the devil with pen and ink," while clinging to the belief that "for every letter and line [copied], a sin is forgiven me."[31]

Many monasteries included a room called a scriptorium where monk copyists called scribes worked. The scriptorium was furnished with specially constructed tables where scribes sat, either on a stool or on their knees, to copy ancient works. Each table had a wooden holder for the page being copied, a sloping desk surface for the fresh page, and a small area for tools. These tools included quills from swans, geese, or crows; ink pots; a small knife called a penknife for sharpening quills; and a compass used to regulate the spaces between letters, words, and lines.

Sitting at his desk, each scribe determined the correct spacing between letters and their size, then dipped his quill in the ink pot. Slowly and meticulously, he copied page after page. The tip of the quill gradually spread with use, requiring the scribe to sharpen the tip every eight or ten letters. If a mistake was discovered that could not be corrected, the sheet was destroyed and replaced by a new one. Only because of the efforts of monk scribes, many of the greatest works of Greek and Roman philosophers, dramatists, poets, and historians have survived.

Some scribes developed excellent reputations throughout literate society for the high quality and accuracy of their work. Such monks enjoyed their reputations and strove to perfect their art. Others, however, complained about their working conditions by leaving personal comments in the margins. Some of the more interesting and revealing include, "Only three fingers are writing, but the whole body is suffering," "Finally it is dinner time," "The scribe has a right to the best wine," "My parchment is the roughest in the world," and "I am not sure if the number [I am copying] is 1,000 or 10,000."[32]

As manuscripts gained in popularity, scribes added artistic decorations called illuminations. At first these artistic touches were simple, but over time the decorations became increasingly elaborate and colorful. Eventually, an entirely different group of monks called illuminators specialized in applying the colored ink after the scribe had finished with the words.

The cost for a single high-quality illuminated manuscript exceeded the equivalent of ten years of income for a common worker. The merchant class, however, along with many wealthy nobles, took pride in building private libraries of beautiful books. A large library might contain forty or fifty books, a collection unimaginable two hundred years earlier. The interest in books, and the wisdom found on their pages, spurred a newfound commitment to scholarship and education.

Monasteries and Education

Another lasting contribution that monasteries made to European civilization was a zealous interest in learning and higher education. At a time when the daily struggle to eat and stay alive occupied most people's thoughts and activities, the church committed a select group of monasteries to function as centers of education and related intellectual pursuits.

Initially monastic schools served the needs of the church exclusively. Monks taught the Latin mass to priests and taught them to read Latin translations of the Bible. Monasteries became the domain of theology students studying ancient religions and writing treatises about the role of religion and monasteries in European society.

Students listen attentively as a monk teaches a philosophy class in a monastery. All across Europe, monasteries established themselves as centers of learning.

The study of ancient texts and theological writings encouraged several monasteries to establish schools that would serve as centers for education specifically for oblates, boys studying to become monks. These schools provided instruction in theology, rhetoric, literature, philosophy, and ethics. According to medieval historian Mayke de Jong, this education encouraged the use of Latin and critical thinking:

> Oblates read the Bible and commentaries on it, the works of the church fathers, and the lives of the saints. They were encouraged to speak Latin among themselves in order to improve their understanding of the texts they read. This would also help them formulate dissertations in Latin, and to sharpen their intellects.[33]

Monastery schools became so well respected that wealthy nobles sent their sons to them; they made sizable financial contributions that allowed monks to purchase books, build libraries, fund master scholars, and pay for educational travel to foreign countries. The sons of nobility returned home to administer family businesses, operate trading companies, and derive pleasure from reading and building personal libraries.

Many respected scholars, both secular and clerical, were educated at these monasteries. One was the twelfth-century Cistercian abbot St. Bernard of Clairvaux,

The Italian philosopher and theologian St. Thomas Aquinas was educated in a monastery and later became a monk.

who wrote sermons and treatises on Christian faith, human union with God, and Christian morality. One hundred years later, St. Thomas Aquinas, while a monk at the Monte Cassino monastery in Italy, published acclaimed treatises on the relationship between faith and reason. He later wrote and taught courses about his views on the nature of God and about some of the earliest known principles of physics.

By the late twelfth and early thirteenth centuries, monks had developed more advanced schools called universities that were incorporated with churches. Their curricula became more universal in scope by encompassing many new and more practical academic disciplines. In addition to studies aimed at priests and monks, the curricula included areas of study for secular students such as law, medicine, eco-

Preparing Parchment

*P*reparing fresh parchment skins to replace decaying ones was a constant Opus Dei for scribes working in monasteries. The work kept scribes and their assistants busy because it involved many highly specialized jobs. The process for preparing animal skins varied from place to place. The following is one such process quoted in Christopher De Hamel's book Medieval Craftsmen: Scribes and Illuminators.

1. Skin a goat, lamb, or calf. (Sometimes even a pig, deer, or squirrel).
2. Wash the skin in clear cold running water for 24 hours.
3. Remove the hair of the skin by soaking the skins in wooden or stone vats in a solution of lime and water for 3–10 days.
4. Remove the wet slippery skins and drape them hair-side out over a great curved wood surface, called a beam. Then stand behind the beam, lean forward over the top, and scrape away the hair with a long curved knife with a wooden handle at each end.
5. Flip the skin over and scrape away the residue of clinging flesh. Be careful not to cut through the skin.
6. Degrease the skin with a series of chalk applications to both sides of the wet skin. This repeated dusting with chalk leaches oils from the skin.
7. If there are any small cuts in the skin, sew them up so they will not enlarge during the drying process.
8. Stretch the skin taut on a frame until dry.
9. When it is dry, scrape and shave the skin with fine pumice to smooth the skin. Fluffy little peelings will fall away that can be boiled to make glue.
10. Cut the skin to the desired size.

Students at a medieval university take notes as a monk lectures from a pulpit.

nomics, agriculture, and mathematics. As a result, monasteries became the best early research facilities for all disciplines including medicine, as historian Andrew Dickson White points out:

> The places where medicine could be applied were at first mainly the infirmaries of various monasteries, especially the larger ones of the Benedictine order: these were frequently developed into hospitals. Many monks devoted themselves to such medical studies as were permitted, and sundry church-men and laymen did much to secure and preserve copies of ancient medical treatises.[34]

Besides offering a broader curriculum, universities were different from the monastery schools in a second significant way. To attract the sons of nobility, they were more conveniently located in big-city cathedrals rather than in remote monasteries. By the late twelfth century, universities were attracting students and teachers interested in advanced studies not just from the immediate region but

St. Francis of Assisi gives his cloak to a destitute man. In keeping with the teachings of Jesus, monks administered to the needs of the poor.

from all over Europe. Europe's first universities in Paris, Bologna, Oxford, and Lisbon attracted Europe's brightest minds, and some offered specialized courses: law in Bologna and Rome, medicine in Salerno, and theology in Paris. Many graduates went on to successful careers in the church, while others entered a variety of secular professions to the benefit of European society.

Traditions of scholarship, libraries, schools, and universities established by monasteries created a precedent of enormous value to later generations by firmly establishing the importance of intellectual inquiry. Yet monastic contributions took other forms beyond the library or classroom. At a time when national governments were incapable of assisting the poor and the sick, monasteries opened their doors to help as many suffering and destitute people as possible.

Caring for the Poor

Poverty was one of the great curses of the Late Middle Ages. Peasant families that fell ill or lost their crops had no expectation for financial assistance. Roads cluttered with beggar families were commented on by numerous travelers, as were entire villages that became ghost towns because of disease, locusts, or droughts that destroyed wheat fields and starved livestock. In times of natural disasters, nobility could also be devastated but never to the extent of the peasants, many of whom might starve or freeze to death.

Following the Crusades, the gap between rich and poor became increasingly evident because of the emergence of the affluent merchant class. By the thirteenth century, every large city featured stately palaces owned by powerful families whose fortunes derived from banking, landholdings, shipping, trading, and similar commercial ventures. Outside these baronial palaces, those who were desperately poor stared in hoping for a few copper coins or pieces of discarded food from those who had so much.

Sympathetic and morally obligated to help the dispossessed, monks took it upon themselves to provide the first organized charitable relief for those most in need. Assisting the poor and homeless was perceived to be an *Opus Dei* in keeping with the biblical tradition of Jesus, who fed the poor, sheltered the homeless, and healed the sick.

Feeding the poor took place daily in most monasteries. Early each morning an amount of bread was designated as alms-bread for the poor. As the sun rose, a somber procession of monks walked from the kitchen to the monastery gate carrying bread, beer (which was cleaner than water), and occasionally soup to distribute to the local poor who gathered there. In addition to the usual provisions, dinner scraps from the previous night were also sent out. Better quality foods were distributed on holy days when monks feasted. Regardless of the amount of food provided, it was never enough for everyone. Hunger was a never-ending problem, as one monastery's abbot, Peter the Venerable, expressed: "There is always a crowd of guests, and the number of poor people is innumerable."[35]

Peasant families were the most vulnerable to economic reverses that resulted in hunger and homelessness. They rarely owned their dwellings, and when crops failed, they sometimes found themselves evicted. Monks were sympathetic to the homeless and worked to assist them by opening spare rooms. This gesture was in keeping with the biblical story of the birth of Jesus in a barn because no inns had rooms for his parents.

In response to the more pathetic plight of homeless children, either abandoned by their parents or orphaned, monks opened orphanages to care for them. Some of the more enlightened monasteries during the eleventh century also required the monks to educate the children, as twelfth-century writer Anna Comnena noted in her journal:

> The children who had lost their parents and were afflicted with the bitter evil of orphanhood were sent to the abbots of the holy monasteries with orders to bring them up, not as slaves, but as free children and allow them a thorough education and instruction in the Holy Writings.[36]

The *Opus Dei* unique to monasteries gradually changed European culture. Concern for the well-being of the suffering poor, combined with intellectual pursuits and exploring new as well as ancient ideas, gradually ushered in a new era in Europe. For the first time in more than five hundred years, two new attitudes emerged: a general optimism about the human spirit and improving people's lives coupled with the notion that solutions to people's personal problems could be found beyond the church.

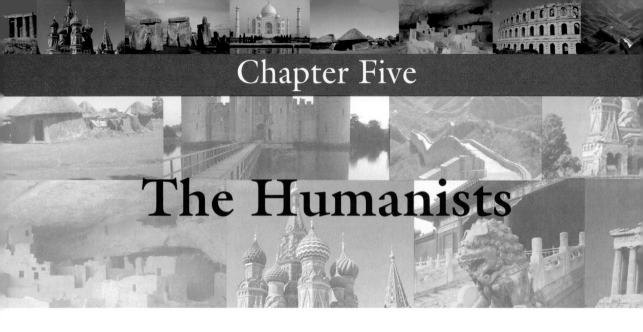

Chapter Five

The Humanists

The cultural and spiritual grip that the Catholic Church exercised over all Europeans was challenged at the beginning of the fourteenth century. Unlike a powerful king, an invading army, or another religion, the challenger this time was a point of view called humanism.

Humanism was a secular philosophy that collided with the teachings of the church. Humanist philosophers, in contradiction to papal teachings, placed humankind at the center of the world rather than God, and stressed the practical world over the divine and mystical powers emphasized by the church. Humanists underscored the importance of human beings here on earth rather than in the afterlife and presented a more optimistic and cheerful outlook. They focused their attention on people's interests, achievements, capabilities, and material needs in this life by emphasizing the notion that pleasure and beauty could be found in the living world. In the opinion of historian Steven

Kreis, "Almost everywhere, humanism began as a rather pious, timid, and conservative drift away from medieval Christianity and ended in bold independence of medieval tradition."[37]

This revolutionary view was not a renunciation of God or a denial of the afterlife but, rather, an acceptance of both. Yet it tipped the balance away from the church's focus on accepting suffering on earth to achieve happiness in heaven toward the humanist focus of achieving happiness while still alive.

Since the inception of Christianity more than a thousand years earlier, people took small comfort in their short and brutish lives hoping for a better life in the afterworld as promised by the church. Many lived in accordance with strict church teachings, paid their Sunday offerings, obeyed the parish priests, and followed the teachings of the Bible—all in hopes of attaining the reward of eternal bliss in heaven. Over time, however, fewer seemed

Humanists taught that humankind, and not God, was the center of the universe, as this manuscript page suggests.

willing to postpone personal happiness. For those people, humanism provided a more cheerful view of life than that offered by the church.

The humanist point of view found expression in a variety of forms. Scholars renewed interest in intellectual inquiry and studied Greek and Roman philosophers; writers for the first time in hundreds of years told stories about people experiencing the emotions of joy and love mixed with sadness and sorrow. Painters depicted the major celebrations of life in scenes of marriages, family gatherings, and births, while sculptors carved famous men and women. Beginning first in Italy and gradually spreading north, humanism provided Europeans with a fresh outlook on life far more optimistic than what early medieval people had experienced. It was, from the point of view of Fremantle, "the intellectual climax of the medieval era."[38]

Rediscovery of the Individual

One major element of the humanist movement was the rediscovery of individualism, a notion that originated in Greece and later spread to Rome but disappeared during the Early Middle Ages. To humanists, individual actions, thoughts, expressions, and beliefs were to be encouraged and admired. These things were out of favor in the church, however, and repressed within the rigid class system that arose under feudalism.

The humanist movement inspired an interest in science and learning. Here, a mathematician, an astronomer, and a scribe are shown at work.

During the Early Middle Ages, the church stressed the view that individualism promoted selfish behavior, insubordination, and sinful behavior. Medieval Christianity fostered the renunciation of one's own interests in favor of the interests of others, and required unquestioning obedience. Catholicism restricted individual expression by demanding that all parishioners uniformly pray, observe church holy days, and accept all church doctrine in the same way and without question.

The rigid feudal system was no more tolerant of individualism than the church. In feudalism, a single individual had little standing. Individuals existed mainly as a member of a group, whether noble, peasant, or priestly. Peasants were expected to work at the same jobs as their parents, never leave the villages where they were born, wear traditional clothes, and honor their feudal contracts. Their activities were determined by law and custom. Any individual who dared challenge authority and customs was either punished or alienated from the community.

The distinction between the notion of the individual during the Early Middle Ages and later during the humanist movement was highlighted in 1860 by the Swiss historian Jacob Burckhardt. He published a book that modern historians consider a masterpiece of scholarship titled *The Civilization of the Renaissance in Italy*. In this work, Burckhardt points out that during the earlier period the individual was merely a member of some vague group but during the later period individuality was honored just as it had been in ancient Greek society:

Peter Abelard

One of the earliest and most respected of the humanist thinkers was the Frenchman Peter Abelard. He was born in 1079 but nothing is known about his life until he studied rhetoric at several church schools in Chartres and Paris when he was in his twenties. Suffering a serious illness in Paris, Abelard moved to the coast of Brittany, where he turned to theology. In 1113 he returned to Paris to teach the subject.

While in Paris, Abelard met Heloise, the most famous female scholar of the Middle Ages. He taught her logic and she taught him about the ancient Greek philosophers Plato and Socrates. The two fell in love and secretly lived together until her uncle discovered their relationship and had Abelard castrated.

Abelard withdrew to the abbey of St. Denis, where he became a monk. Although he was well disciplined, he was too restless and too argumentative for the monastic life. In 1121 he published a humanist theological work, *On the Divine Unity and Trinity*, but it was burned at an ecclesiastical council at Soissons. Undaunted, Abelard founded a school in 1125 and then returned to Paris to continue his humanist teaching.

As one of the principal humanist thinkers, Abelard believed that something had to be understood before it could be believed. He proposed a division between faith and knowledge because faith alone did not answer most questions about the world. He believed that doubting led to inquiry and inquiry led to wisdom. By comparing arguments and choosing the best among them, one could come to truth.

Abelard retired to Cluny, where he died in 1142 and was buried with Heloise.

In the Middle Ages . . . Man was conscious of himself as a member of a race, people, party, family, or corporation—only through some general category. In Italy this veil first melted into air; an objective treatment and consideration of the state and of all the things of this world became possible. Man became a spiritual individual, and recognized himself as such. In the same way, the Greek distinguished himself from the barbarian.[39]

In keeping with the Greek sense of optimism about individual possibilities, humanists encouraged curiosity and innovative points of view. At the center of the movement was the growing desire for knowledge and love of learning. Healthy skepticism proposed by individual thinkers nourished new ideas about tearing down the rigid social structure and challenging the mysticism of the church. Individual experiences on earth became of greater interest than the uncertainty of the afterlife.

The earliest intellectual group to express the principles of humanism was the writers. Early humanist writers rejected the Early Middle Ages as primitive and backward and looked to the time of the ancient Greeks and Romans for inspiration.

The Emergence of a New Literary Genre

Early humanist writers were captivated by the secular outlook of the Greeks and Romans. In keeping with the principles of humanism, scholars first reveled in the works of the ancient Greeks and Romans and then moved forward to create a new literary genre that emphasized everyday life experiences, celebrated the emotional and social lives of people, and gradually moved away from stories based on church doctrine.

The humanists were attracted to the writers of antiquity rather than those of

Dante Alighieri stands between Purgatory and the city of Florence in this painting of the Divine Comedy, *Dante's literary masterpiece.*

Petrarch believed that true intellectualism could only be gained by studying the writings of the ancients.

Christianity because, like themselves, they were relatively uninterested in the spiritual world and afterlife. They were more interested in a happy and contented life on earth. Humanists studied and copied Greek philosophy because it instructed humans on how to find life satisfying rather than how to gain access to heaven after death. Anne Fremantle notes that humanist writers "glorified the sensuous and worldly life . . . filled with good and evil and accepted all conditions of men as they were."[40]

One of the earliest humanist writers, the Italian Dante Alighieri (1265–1321), lived during a time of transition in his hometown of Florence. Dante was a man of considerable learning. His masterpiece, the *Divine Comedy*, describes his imaginative travels through hell, purgatory, and heaven. It is the earliest major work written in Italian rather than Latin, the language of medieval scholars and church officials exclusively, because Dante wanted as many common people as possible to read it.

The lengthy work combines Dante's vast knowledge of classical Latin writers and Greek philosophers with his readings from the religious and theological classics of Catholicism. In this regard, the use of classical and Christian writers side by side, one of the hallmarks of the humanist movement, was an insult to Christian ideals because the Greeks and Romans were not Christians. The *Divine Comedy* also reflects the author's sense that the church and state are of equal importance, a concept that caused him to be exiled from Florence by the city's bishop. The book also expresses his disgust with the corruption of the church by politics during his lifetime. While traveling through hell, for example, Dante meets many of the corrupt popes and describes the horrific punishments each faces.

After Dante, Petrarch (1304–1374) is regarded as the greatest of the early humanist writers. Petrarch's contribution to the Late Middle Ages was his emphasis on the virtues of intellectual freedom and individual expression as had been practiced by the Roman writers Virgil and Cicero. Petrarch wrote extensively, producing poetry, biographies of historical figures, and scores of letters to his lover, Laura.

Petrarch was more thoroughly committed to humanism than was Dante. To Petrarch, intellectual interest could be found only in ancient writings, not in those of the church. He located manuscripts of the classics; collected Greek and Roman

The Queen of Cathedrals

Fifty miles south of Paris, one of the greatest examples of Gothic architecture rose high above the wheat fields of Chartres. Primarily constructed between 1194 and 1220, the cathedral continued to be modified with decorative additions for hundreds of years. Art historians widely consider this cathedral to be Europe's quintessential example of Gothic architecture and have dubbed it the "queen of cathedrals."

Its most noticeable architectural feature is the two tall spires that rise high above the cathedral roof and can be seen from miles away. Twin matching spires are a common feature in the Gothic style, but what makes these spires unique is that each displays a distinctly different design. The shorter of the two, 349 feet tall, is a simple pyramid form, but the taller, which was added four hundred years after the first, rises 377 feet and is far more ornate.

The single most striking architectural interior feature of the cathedral is the large circular stained-glass windows set into the towering stone walls. They were designed to provide splashes of interior color and light, the only light illuminating the cavernous interior with the exception of candles. The large delicate windows escaped damage during numerous wars between the thirteenth and twentieth centuries. The thousands of individual pieces of stained glass constitute one of the most complete collections of medieval stained glass in the world and bathe the interior with a blue tint.

Structurally the cathedral has survived intact because of its superb arches and vaults that support the heavy roof made of stone and covered with copper and slate. The interior arches and vaults carry the weight of the roof and transmit it to the outer walls, which are prevented from buckling by the exterior flying buttresses that stabilize them.

coins; and when he went to Rome, visited the ancient archaeological sites rather than holy ones.

Petrarch also studied Aristotle's thoughts on logic and concluded—along with other humanists—that humans are capable of rational thought and the world can be logically understood by reason. Persons endowed with reason can understand their lives and the universe within a logical framework without the need of illogical church doctrine that often inaccurately represented the realities of nature and human behavior.

Humanists also believed that beauty could afford some glimpse into what heaven might be like. This sense of aesthetics, which was rarely of interest to people in earlier times, gradually found an appreciative audience in the Late Middle Ages.

The Color and Grace of Gothic Architecture

A physical manifestation of the humanist call for greater beauty was a new form of architecture called Gothic. Tall, elegant, ornately decorated, and colorful, hundreds of Gothic cathedrals were built throughout Europe between the early eleventh and late fourteenth centuries. Kreis explains that the phenomenon of magnificent Gothic architecture was founded in the

With its soaring spires and enormous stained glass medallion window, the cathedral of Chartres is one of the finest examples of Gothic architecture in Europe.

humanist passion for beauty: "Beauty was believed to afford at least some glimpse of a transcendental existence. This goes far to explain the humanist cult of beauty and makes plain that humanism was, above everything else, fundamentally an aesthetic movement."[41]

During the Early Middle Ages, churches were of the Romanesque architectural style characterized by squat dimensions, thick stone and concrete walls, and very few windows for light. Inside, somber darkness prevailed even at midday despite burning candles. The lack of lighting was so commonplace that interior decorations were never attempted. This architectural style reflected the use of the church as a place of worship and a place of defense against invading armies; beauty and elegance were not considerations during those troubled times. But as the Late Middle Ages moved forward and people yearned for greater beauty and comfort while worshipping, humanist architects and engineers experimented with new techniques to make cathedrals more appealing to the eye and to illuminate their interiors with splashes of color. In the opinion of art historian George Holmes,

> The construction of Chartres [Cathedral] at the end of the twelfth century led this style [Gothic] that became so dominant and its monuments so impressive that they have come for many to symbolize the Middle Ages generally and the humanist movement in particular. In art, as in other aspects, the French looked forward to an increasingly changing world.[42]

Individualized and highly detailed statutes of the apostles decorate the entryway of Chartres Cathedral.

Beginning in France and then spreading throughout Europe, graceful Gothic cathedrals rose high above the landscape. With an eye for creating more graceful structures for worshippers, architects added tall spires to the roofs; the walls became taller and thinner, giving them an elegant appearance; and large circular stained-glass windows were added to flood the cavernous interiors with light. All of these features reflected the new sense of joy and optimism introduced by humanists.

These new features were a challenge to engineers. Tall, thin walls pierced by glass windows occasionally buckled outward and collapsed under the weight of heavy roofs. The great cathedral of Notre Dame in Paris, which took two hundred years to complete, collapsed while under construction, killing more than one hundred workmen. Other cathedral collapses had similar results. To remedy the problem of buckling walls, engineers studied Roman manuscripts describing the support systems for large buildings and invented external supports called flying buttresses. Flying buttresses were exterior arches placed against walls to stabilize them.

In addition to the buttressing, beautifully carved interior marble columns were added from floor to ceiling.

Bathed in light, the interiors of Gothic cathedrals were decorated to delight parishioners. Entire walls were covered with murals, tapestries, and mosaics

Donatello's marble statue of Saint John the Baptist emphasizes the true proportions of the human body.

depicting commonly understood religious scenes. As the Late Middle Ages continued, cathedral interiors became increasingly ornate and colorful, two qualities that brought a dimension of enjoyment to religious services.

Sculpting Biblical and Pagan Heroes

The rise of Gothic architecture led to the development of a new style of sculpture. Gothic sculptors began decorating the columns, entryways, and arches of Gothic cathedrals. Early sculptural forms such as those carved into stone surfaces were called low-relief because the carvings were only a few inches deep. Typical early low-relief carvings portrayed large numbers of anonymous biblical figures tightly packed together as a stiff, blocky group.

As the demand for sculpture increased, sculptors mastered their craft. They experimented with freestanding sculptures representing single biblical figures that stood on pedestals. These three-dimensional figures allowed admirers to walk around them and view them from all sides. This revolutionary form demanded that sculptors study human anatomy to understand how individual parts of the body adjust and move to maintain proper balance.

As sculptors improved, they made their forms more lifelike. Carving marble and molding bronze, sculptors subscribing to humanist principles celebrated the human form by adding the depiction of movement to their figures. In contrast to earlier works that had appeared stiff and lifeless, biblical figures were depicted walking, turning, and gesturing. By the beginning of the fourteenth century, sculpture developed graceful lines showing twisting torsos and fluid movement.

One of the great sculptors of the Late Middle Ages was the Italian Donatello (1386–1466). He was one of the first medieval sculptors to pursue an attitude toward the human body similar to that of the Greeks and Romans, one that stressed exact proportion and the appearance of fluid movement. Art historian H.W. Janson made this observation about Donatello's emulation of earlier master sculptors:

The man who did most to re-establish this attitude was Donatello, the greatest sculptor of his time. . . . In a performance that truly marks an epic, the young Donatello has mastered at one stroke the central achievement of ancient sculpture. He treats the body as an articulated structure, capable of movement.[43]

Toward the end of Donatello's career, he and fellow sculptors working in Florence took humanism to new heights. They moved further from the church's influence by creating nonbiblical figures in marble and bronze. Sculptures depicting mythical champions such as St. George and Classical figures such as Hercules, Zeus, and Poseidon began to dot the piazzas of Italian cities.

Painting Emotional Themes

Embracing the humanist ideal that people are of central importance, artists of the Late Middle Ages gradually shifted their focus from depicting generally dark, somber, and dispassionate biblical scenes to depicting common people expressing emotions toward one another. Painting on canvas, wood, and plaster walls, artists illustrated people going about their daily lives, playing with their children, or attending wedding ceremonies. The more painters perfected their craft, the more the faces and bodies they painted achieved greater realism. They became more accurately proportioned, and of greater importance the facial expressions for the first time revealed inner feelings.

The painter most recognized as transcending the cold and stiff depictions of the Early Middle Ages was the Florentine Giotto (1267–1337). In the late thirteenth century when Giotto was a teenager, he studied with the master painter Cimabue and within two years exceeded his teacher's abilities. Giotto's paintings were revolutionary because the figures in them conveyed emotions. Although his subjects were biblical figures, as had been the tradition for hundreds of years, they were depicted with smiles, frowns, and tears.

Giotto gained fame for the expressive painting of the Three Wise Men in the fresco at the Arena Chapel in Padua, Italy. Each man's face reveals a different emotion as he looks at the baby Jesus. One face expresses excitement, another confusion, and the third astonishment. This painting even shows the surprised smiling face of a camel looking down in joy at the newly born Christ. Suggesting that a camel might express happiness, especially in a painting depicting Christ, would have been considered sacrilegious prior to the humanist movement.

The Dreams of Roger Bacon

One of the greatest earliest humanist thinkers of the thirteenth century was Roger Bacon, who taught at both the University of Paris and Oxford University in England. Bacon is revered even today because he was one of the earliest men of science who admonished students to lay aside the books of the old Greek and Roman intellectuals and make their own scientific discoveries using careful experiments and scrupulously accurate observations.

Bacon committed all of his energy and family fortune to studying science. Of particular interest to him were mathematics, optics, and engineering sciences. He bought books, equipment, instruments, and mathematical tables. These were all very expensive because all books were in manuscript form and each volume had to be copied by hand.

Bacon was one of the earliest medieval thinkers to investigate and conjecture about a variety of scientific ideas, going so far as to propose that someday science would outdo the wonders of magic. Bacon was a master at careful observation and concluded, among other things, that great oceangoing ships with just one man steering them would one day go faster than if they were filled with rowers. He predicted that wagons would one day move with incredible speed without being pulled by oxen. He also predicted, long before Leonardo da Vinci, that machines would be built that would allow humans to fly like a bird.

Considered by art historians as the most dramatic example of Giotto's paintings is a work called the *Kiss of Judas*. This painting highlights the moment when Christ confronts Judas, who will soon kiss him to identify him to the Romans who wish to arrest him. Surrounded by dark and fiery symbols of conflict and chaos, the painting is filled with emotion as Judas leans forward to kiss Christ. The two men stand face to face. Judas has a tense worried look as he leans in for the kiss but looks away. Christ, on the other hand, looks down directly into the eyes of Judas with a stern yet calm expression, signaling his premonition of the betrayal. In the background, Giotto painted waving torches and wooden clubs to underscore the tension between the two men.

A variety of circumstances, some from within the church and some from without, caused people to replace their view of the world as defined by the church with the new humanist view. The principle taught by the church, that life has importance only for determining one's afterlife, gradually lost interest for many Europeans. Tuchman comments on this by observing, "The rupture of this principle and its replacement with the worth of the individual and of an active life not necessarily focused on God is, in fact, what created the modern world and ended the middle ages."[44]

Chapter Six

The Emergence of the Nation-State

By roughly the late thirteenth and early fourteenth centuries, much of Europe had outgrown the feudal system. The relatively simple agrarian economy, the scattering of decentralized villages, and the need for protection by warlords that had once justified feudalism began to give way to modern complexities that feudalism could no longer manage. A general calm descended on Europe, encouraged by international trade, the accumulation of wealth, a realization that warfare had to subside, and the optimistic spirit of humanism that promised greater personal freedom and satisfaction. As these major forces and many secondary ones took hold, European civilization experienced profound social changes that redefined the relationships between the classes, diminished the role of the church, and introduced judicial and economic systems. These changes required a modern system of governance more complex and sophisticated than feudalism.

An infusion of money was one of the catalysts that introduced change. Large sums of money began to circulate, and mercantile families amassed great fortunes. Surpluses of money allowed these people, who were neither nobles nor peasants, to live luxurious lives and to defy the nobility. Thriving new businesses in turn drew some farmers to energetic city life, caused blighted villages to become vibrant towns, and forced fragmented governments to promulgate new laws to cope with the increasing legal and social complexities of a new era. The poor

This tenth-century gold piece bears the likeness of the Byzantine ruler Constantine VII.

A merchant counts his earnings on a table. With the introduction of currency in the Late Middle Ages, a number of mercantile families amassed huge fortunes.

and middle-income families seemed to benefit from the infusion of money the most and the nobility the least.

The nobility, however, felt the threat of change the most. As the need for protection subsided, the nobility had difficulty justifying their place within the feudal social structure. They were generally resented and feared by the peasants, and the mercantile class of wealthy business-men treated them with disdain. Over time, their authority plummeted in the eyes of everyone because they no longer made a contribution to the common good.

As the nobility were shunted aside by peasants and merchants alike, they turned against their kings. Aware that their role in society was diminishing, the nobles made demands on the kings to allow them to play a stronger role in their country's policies. To those kings who had become accustomed to ruling with absolute authority, such demands were an annoyance. Nonetheless, new tensions between kings and the upper nobility were evidence of serious social conflict.

Farsighted leaders saw these changing conditions and began the gradual process of defining a new political institution to administer them called the nation-state, the precursor of today's modern nations. But before any new revolutionary ideas could be implemented, many old ones would first need to be swept aside.

Limiting Kings' Absolute Authority

Hoping to strengthen their role, rebellious nobility in the thirteenth century managed to wring out a series of landmark concessions from a handful of kings. Kings had angered the nobility for generations because of ill-conceived foreign wars costing the lives of thousands, disastrous fiscal policies necessitating higher taxes, capriciously applied laws, and arrogant attitudes excluding the nobility from major decisions. Although several kingdoms experienced these skirmishes between the privileged and their absolute rulers, they were the most pronounced in England.

An event in 1215 triggered the first showdown between a king and his nobility. Angered by the reckless behavior of King John following a crushing defeat at the hands of the

French, a group of English nobility confronted him at the town of Runnymede beside the Thames River. Threatening him with civil war if he refused to hear their grievances, the nobles drew up their armies and awaited his response. Rather than risk war, John agreed to affix his seal to a list of demands called the Articles of the Barons, and later the Magna Carta, a Latin term meaning the "Great Charter."

The Magna Carta established for the first time that the power of the king could be limited. In this charter, the lords

A king sits on his throne as he dictates to his scribe a new set of laws for his realm.

demanded greater rights for the nobility in determining law and placed specific restrictions on the authority of the king. For the first time in European history, the king was placed under the laws of the land, no longer above them. Never before had a European king been limited by a binding contract with the weight of law. Forcing John to agree to the Magna Carta, which contradicted the feudal custom that forbade the nobility from exercising authority over the king, was one of the early indications that feudalism was becoming a relic from the past.

Pictured here is a page from the Magna Carta, which limited the power of King John of England.

The Magna Carta contained sixty-three paragraphs specifying changes and new limitations to the king's authority. Those with the most far-reaching consequences included the condition that the king could no longer raise taxes without the approval of the nobility, seize private property without compensation, or imprison citizens without first giving them a fair trial. The Magna Carta was copied and sent to major cities throughout England for all to read.

Concessions such as the Magna Carta strengthened the hand of the nobility, but their improved condition was temporary. The decline of kings' authority, however, was permanent. In fact, the general decline of feudalism was showing signs of being irreversible.

The Decline of Feudalism

By the fourteenth century, the major reasons for the emergence of feudalism were largely lost. Kings had finally established strong loyal armies able to deter foreign invaders, and the emerging merchant class of traders, bankers, and a variety of entrepreneurs no longer fit into the aging and rigid feudal model of the duty-bound relationship between the peasantry and nobility.

The notion of homage and fealty that once held feudal society together was gradually rendered meaningless by several significant changes. Fewer wars, the introduction of money, and cosmopolitan centers acting as magnets for rural populations finally provided the peasantry with a degree of mobility. Peasants were no longer forced to remain in the same village

Witnesses to the Black Plague

In the spring of 1348, dockworkers at northern Italian seaports gave little thought to the rats that scurried off boats. They were a regular yet inconsequential pest associated with trading ships. But this time the rats carried diseased fleas that within three years would bite and wipe out one-third of Europe's population. Several eyewitness accounts of the disease known as the Black Plague can be found on the Web site Insecta Inspecta World.

How many valiant men, how many fair ladies, breakfast with their kinfolk and the same night supped with their ancestors in the next world? The condition of the people was pitiable to behold. They sickened by the thousands daily, and died unattended and without help. Many died in the open street, others dying in their houses, made it known by the stench of their rotting bodies. Consecrated churchyards did not suffice for the burial of the vast multitude of bodies, which were heaped by the hundreds in vast trenches, like goods in a ships hold and covered with a little earth.
—Giovanni Boccaccio

Realizing what a deadly disaster had come to them the people quickly drove the Italians from their city. However, the disease remained, and soon death was every where. Fathers abandoned their sick sons. Lawyers refused to come and make out wills for the dying. Friars and nuns were left to care for the sick, and monasteries and convents were soon deserted, as they were stricken, too. Bodies were left in empty houses, and there was no one to give them a Christian burial.
—Unknown

as their parents and grandparents and exchange their goods and services for protection. For the first time in hundreds of years, peasants could leave home to live in other villages, buy their own land, find work in more exciting urban centers, or simply sell their wares and foods directly to the general public.

As the relationship between nobles and peasants changed, the nobility lost importance. Its gradual obsolescence was largely of its own making. Young knights were willing to pledge their fidelity to multiple lords in hopes of acquiring extra land but were unwilling to fight for all of them. On occasion, a local war broke out, forcing the knight to choose between two of his lords. Such unethical arrangements subverted the original feudal ideal of personal loyalty between lord and vassal. Equally to be blamed were the sons of noblemen who refused to go off to war at all. By paying sculage, a tax releasing them from their military obligations, they avoided battle.

Wat Tyler (lower left) is struck down by one of the king's men in 1381. Tyler's revolt was precipitated by an unfair poll tax levied by the king.

Over time, professional armies arose that fought for pay rather than feudal obligation. When the mercenaries, especially the mounted knights, returned from war, they demanded entry to the nobility. This sequence of events diluted the nobility so much that it gradually lost much of its former prestige.

Feudalism's decline was also rooted in ties to family. Family ties came to be seen as more important than territorial or protective obligations. Respect for historically based ties between lord and vassal steadily weakened as the economic and social gulf between greater and lesser nobles grew wider. These circumstances also contributed to the destruction of feudalism, slowly and inevitably as historian J. Michael Beasley noted (paraphrasing historian J.J. Bagley):

The 14th century marked the end of the true feudal age and began paving the way for strong monarchies, nation states, and national wars. It [feudalism] was ceasing to belong to the real world of practical living. Much 14th century feudalism had become artificial and self-conscious. Already men were finding it a little curious. It was acquiring an antiquarian interest and losing its usefulness.[45]

Around the mid–fourteenth century, no societal class was more enthusiastic about contributing to the decline of feudalism than the peasants. As signs of decay became increasingly apparent, peasants organized to rise up against the nobility that had oppressed them for centuries.

Peasant Revolts

The spreading breakdown of the feudal social and political order inevitably led to

The English Peasants' Revolt of 1381

Tensions between peasants and the nobility were constant for a variety of reasons. One ongoing source of conflict was unreasonable taxation foisted on the peasants by the nobility. In 1381 a peasant revolt erupted in a village in England and soon spread across the country. It ultimately resulted in some long-range improvements to peasants' living conditions, albeit at the initial cost of many lives.

In 1380 the English poll-tax (a tax on each adult) for the year raised less money than in previous years. The next year, tax collectors were sent out again, this time with instructions to collect more. The poll tax levied in the village of Fobbing was three times the rates of those previously imposed. The tax was particularly grievous for those least able to pay. As a result, peasant anger reached a peak, and a riot erupted during which the tax collectors were beaten and driven from the village.

Word of the riot in Fobbing spread. Peasants in neighboring towns banded together and turned on their landowners. Manor houses were burned down and tax records destroyed. Soon uprisings exploded in many other areas of the country. Some landowners were killed, others fled, and still others were beaten and humiliated by being forced to act as servants and perform menial tasks.

In June 1381 Wat Tyler and John Ball led an estimated fifty thousand rebels on a march to London. The peasants intended to explain their grievances to the king, who would, they hoped, grant them a series of reforms. The king pretended to agree to the demands just to get the peasants to return to their villages. Once they departed, the king reneged on his agreement and ordered the deaths of all rebel leaders. The hated poll tax, however, was never again collected and lords treated the peasants with much more respect.

peasant uprisings and resistance. The peasantry found itself caught between its own hard times and the obligations it still owed to the lord of the manor. Adding insult to injury for the peasantry was the appearance that the lifestyle of the upper class had actually improved while theirs had declined; starvation and sickness were commonplace yet workers were still expected to maintain their workloads. This was especially true following the Black Death that killed one-third of the population of Europe between 1348 and 1351.

Toward the middle of the fourteenth century, peasant uprisings sporadically erupted across Europe. The first major uprising occurred in France in 1356, followed by one in Italy in 1378, and England in 1381. Each uprising began in a small village where the peasants united to express common discontent. But as news of the uprisings traveled down the roads, other villagers suffering similar hardships and feeling the same resentment took up shovels and other tools to attack local castles and manor houses and murder the nobility.

Violence was not the only tactic peasants used to express their discontent. In some villages peasants joined forces and refused to provide their labor obligations, while in others they worked very slowly or completed the work improperly. Realizing that there was little they could do to force their peasants to work harder or better, some nobles allowed their workers to purchase releases from their contracts. Once freed from their contractual obligations, peasants paid rent for their land and received wages for their work.

The impact of peasant revolts was noticeable and immediate. Each country responded to them differently, but the general tone was one of conciliation out of fear that more uprisings might erupt. The upper class understood that its survival was based on the willingness of the lower class to continue working. For the first time, many kings taxed the nobility and merchants but not the peasantry. Kings also responded to the grievance that the judicial system was corrupt, inconsistently imposed, and unfairly oppressive toward the poor.

A Modern Judicial System

Justice became one of the keys necessary for improved government, peace, and security in the Late Middle Ages. England, France, Italy, and Germany were the first nations to tackle the problem of unfair, irrational, and inconsistently applied justice. Leaders of the four nations, influenced by humanist principles, recognized the need for judicial systems to move away from groundless ideas about divine intervention, as in the cases of trials by combat. Instead, they began to support rationally based and uniformly applied laws guided by evidence, investigation, a jury of peers, and examination and cross-examination of the accused.

The implementation of modern judicial systems, based on Roman law, motivated lawyers and judges to experiment with demonstrations of evidence, proof, the testimony of witnesses, and the use of juries. England's King Henry II introduced the concept of the twelve-man jury system. After questioning twelve men about a dispute and finding all twelve in agreement, Henry pronounced the unanimous results to be *vere dictu—*, Latin for "truly spoken," from which the English legal term *verdict* eventually evolved.

To meet the growing desire to find legal solutions to controversies instead of fighting to determine their outcome, courts were forced to make themselves more efficient. As the courts tried more cases, they gained valuable experience that aided in the development of good legal procedures based on precedent, cross-examination of witnesses, and evidence that raised judicial standards for consistency and fairness.

As many aging remnants of feudalism gave way to more modern notions of individual rights and freedoms, the antiquated monetary system based on land and feudal contracts slowly faded. Taking its

In this fifteenth-century illustration, French merchants haggle over the price of imported goods near the port of a walled city.

A capitalist economy afforded opportunities for small businessmen, such as this fish vendor, to thrive.

place was a modern economic system based on individual wealth and private ownership.

The Rise of Capitalism

Gradual failures within feudal institutions near the end of the Late Middle Ages gave rise to a new economic system that eclipsed manorialism. The new economic system called capitalism was based on private ownership of land and businesses and the use of money, known as capital, for all business transactions instead of trading.

The rise of capitalism first required breaking the bonds of feudalism and manorialism. By the fourteenth century, signs of decline were evident. The most notable changes were the advent of wage labor, private ownership of land, freedom to travel to find new homes and employment, equitable judicial systems, distribution of coinage, widespread trade, and the disintegration of the rigid class system. These changes provided millions of people with improved economic opportunities.

Europe's entire economy grew under capitalism. Some poor families pooled their money, began small businesses, and shared the profits. Each time small businessmen made money and invested it back into their company, their businesses grew. Weavers, jewelers, furniture makers, bakers, shoemakers, wagon makers, tavern owners, and an assortment of other business owners who experienced success hired more workers, bought new and improved equipment, and expanded their business bases. Gradually, the small one- or two-employee businesses associated with feudalism and manorialism gave way to larger companies offering a greater variety of goods than ever before.

In addition to accumulating capital and expanding businesses, entrepreneurs developed more sophisticated banking transactions and business payment systems needed for emerging capitalism. No longer could businessmen risk transporting bags full of gold and silver coins to make purchases. Instead, for the first time, payments for goods were made using what was called an exchange of credit, a promissory note to pay for goods at a later time. One such note between a Belgian and Italian businessman specified, "I Hans Olbrechts, have received goods from you,

Giovanni Cipolla, at Bruges, October 1, 1353, to the value of 1,000 ducats and I promise to pay you 1,100 ducats by July 1, 1354."[46] As this written contract indicates, the agreement between the two men was more than an exchange of credit; it was also a nine-month loan at an annual interest rate of 12.5 percent. Loans such as this further stimulated businesses by extending capital to people with an immediate need to purchase goods but without the immediate ability to pay for them.

For the first time in nearly a thousand years, the gap between rich and poor began to close. The peasant class, which included most Europeans, began to understand that they could make choices that would have been unimaginable to their ancestors. Workers, unlike their ancestors, were now able to choose their professions rather than being locked into them, as had been the case for many generations. Successful merchants, denied access to the nobility because they were not born into it, were able to purchase finer homes than many nobles and for the first time took an active role in local politics. Families with modest incomes sent their sons to school, where they sat beside the sons of the lower nobility, and over time the two groups learned to work together.

Profile of the Nation-State

Major changes gradually led to the emergence of what many historians refer to as the modern nation-state. The rise of justice systems, capitalism, and mobility within the class system swept away feudalism and ushered in a new age in which kings shared power with those they ruled.

Eyewitness to the French Peasants' Revolt

Many eyewitness reports of the French Peasants' Revolt exist, but few are more poignant than those in The Chronicles of Froissart *(edited by G.C. Macauly). Contained in these records are insights into the resentment and hatred generally felt by the peasants toward the nobility. Froissart wrote:*

Thus they gathered together without any other counsel, and without any armor saving with staves and knives, and so went to the house of a knight dwelling thereby, and broke up his house and slew the knight and the lady and all his children great and small and burnt his house. And they then went to another castle, and took the knight thereof and bound him fast to a stake, and then violated his wife and his daughter before his face and then slew the lady and his daughter and all his other children, and then slew the knight by great torment and burnt and beat down the castle.

And so they did to various other castles and good houses; and they multiplied so that they were six thousand, and ever as they went forward they increased so that every gentleman fled from them and took their wives and children with them, and left their house void and their goods therein.

They destroyed and burnt in the country of Beauvoisin about Corbie, and Amiens and Montdidier more than threescore good houses and strong castles. In like manner these unhappy people were in Brie and Artois, so that all the ladies, knights, and squires of that country fled away to Meaux in Brie, as well the duchess of Normandy and the duchess of Orleans as divers other ladies and damsels, or else they had been violated and after murdered.

The new nation-state differed from the antiquated feudal state in significant ways. By the fourteenth century the geographical boundaries of most nations were defined and recognized by all European citizens and rulers. These borders, primarily drawn along geographical features such as major rivers and mountain ranges, restricted the population over which governments presided and were defended by national armies against intruders.

People for the first time expressed a sense of patriotism to a nation rather than a local province or village. They began referring to themselves as Italian, Swedish, French, English, German, Polish, or Belgian. As travel increased, the many regional languages and varieties of dialects gradually folded together, providing each new nation-state with a common language for the convenience of all citizens.

In this late-fifteenth-century painting, Belgian villagers, lords and ladies, peasants and knights alike, indulge in a lavish celebration.

Germans, for example, traveling throughout their expansive nation during the Early Middle Ages, could expect to encounter six major dialects, each of which contained many subdialects. By the end of the Late Middle Ages, however, the number began to decrease to the point where any traveling German could converse with most other Germans.

The most important component of the emerging nation-state, which was initially resisted by kings but later grudgingly accepted, was a constitutional form of government in which the king remained on his throne but his power was no longer absolute. The Hungarians established their chancellery in 1181 as a legislature to share power with the king; in 1235 Scotland assembled its first Parliament; England established its Parliament in 1265; in 1290 Sweden instituted its State Council; and the French elected their Estates-General in 1302. With one central authority came the control of one centrally administered army pledged to defend the entire nation, the issuance of one form of currency that would be centrally regulated, the establishment of one uniform code of weights and measures applicable to all products sold, and a single law code evenly and impartially applied to all citizens of the nation.

By the waning of the Late Middle Ages, many of the attributes once associated with the rule of the Roman Empire had returned. Greater security was restored, along with vigorous economies, reasonable and equitable application of the law, standardized monetary systems, and relative freedom to travel. However, what made the situation at the end of the Late Middle Ages different from the Roman era was the emergence of many nation-states, each unique, independent, and ruled by some form of constitutional monarchy.

As the people of the Late Middle Ages approached the end of their era, they lived in a world fundamentally much different from that of their ancestors who lived in the beginning of the period. They had moved beyond a dark time of fear and chaotic uncertainty to experience the beginnings of a modern European civilization based on law, representative government, greater individual freedoms, and aspirations unknown to their predecessors. The social and cultural strides made during the Late Middle Ages laid the groundwork for the extraordinary modern civilization enjoyed today by Europeans and Americans alike.

Notes

Introduction: Gradual Awakenings

1. Thomas Asbridge, *The First Crusade: A New History*. Oxford, UK: Oxford University Press, 2004, p. 45.

Chapter 1: The Advent of Feudal Society

2. Quoted in Anne Fremantle, *The Age of Faith*. New York: Time-Life, 1965, p. 14.
3. Quoted in William R. Cook and Ronald B. Herzman, *The Medieval World View*. Oxford, UK: Oxford University Press, 2004, p. 165.
4. Quoted in Frances and Joseph Gies, *Daily Life in Medieval Times*. New York: Black Dog & Leventhal, 1999, p. 12.
5. Norman Cantor, ed., *The Medieval Reader*. New York: HarperCollins, 1994, pp. 3–4.
6. Quoted in E.P. Cheyney, trans., *University of Pennsylvania Translations and Reprints*, vol. 4. Philadelphia: University of Pennsylvania Press, 1898, p. 27.
7. Barbara Tuchman, *A Distant Mirror: The Calamitous 14th Century*. New York: Ballantine, 1978, p. 32.

8. Quoted in Steven Kreis, "European Agrarian Society: Manorialism," *The History Guide*, 2004. www.historyguide. org/ancient/lecture22b.html.
9. Quoted in Stephen Alsford, "History of Medieval Ipswich," 2001. www.trytel. com/~tristan/towns/ipswich6.html.
10. "Crime and Punishment in Elizabethan England," EyeWitness to History, 2001. www.eyewitnessto history.com/punishment.htm.

Chapter 2: Nobility Fighting Nobility

11. Frances Gies, *The Knight in History*. New York: Harper & Row, 1984, p. 12.
12. Quoted in Gies, *Daily Life in Medieval Times*, pp. 100–101.
13. Orderic Vitalis, "The Battle of Hastings According to Orderic Vitalis," in *The Ecclesiastical History of England and Normandy* vol. 2, trans. Thomas Forrester. London: Bohn, 1853. www. shsu.edu/~his_ncp/Orderic.html#n11.
14. Maurice Keen, *Chivalry*. New Haven, CT: Yale University Press, 1984, p. 230.
15. Dave Etheridge, "Welsh Warfare," Regia Anglorum, 2003. www.regia. org/welswar.htm.
16. Quoted in Gies, *Daily Life in Medieval Times*, p. 91.

17. Frank E. Smitha, "Warlords of Europe, to 1050," 2000. www.fsmitha.com/h3/h05eu.htm.

18. Quoted in *Chronique: Journal of Chivalry*, "Knighting Ceremonies," issue 5. www.chronique.com/Chronique/chrniq05.htm#Chronique5g.

Chapter 3: The Crusades and Their Contribution to Europe

19. Gies, *The Knight in History*, p. 35.

20. Quoted in Fremantle, *The Age of Faith*, p. 55.

21. Quoted in Fremantle, *The Age of Faith*, p. 54.

22. Quoted in Paul Halsall, "Peter the Hermit and the Popular Crusade: Collected Accounts," *Internet Medieval Source Book*, December 1997. www.fordham.edu/halsall/source/peterhermit.html.

23. Quoted in Paul Halsall, "Fulcher of Chartres: History of the Expedition to Jerusalem," *Internet Medieval Source Book*, December 1997. www.fordham.edu/halsall/source/fulcher-cde. html.

24. Scott J. Beem, "The (Not So) Poor Knights of the Temple," Eastern Illinois University, Spring 1996. www.eiu.edu/~historia/1997/knights97.htm.

25. Quoted in George Holmes, *The Oxford Illustrated History of Medieval Europe*. Oxford, UK: Oxford University Press, 1990, p. 224.

26. Quoted in Cook and Herzman, *The Medieval World Views*, p. 183.

Chapter 4: Contributions of Pious Brethren

27. Quoted in Fremantle, *The Age of Faith*, p. 38.

28. Fremantle, *The Age of Faith*, p. 38.

29. Matthew 19:21.

30. Quoted in C.H. Lawrence, *Medieval Monasticism*. London: Longman, 2001, p. 1.

31. Quoted in Fremantle, *The Age of Faith*, p. 48.

32. Quoted in Jean Décarreaux, *Monks and Civilization*. trans. Charlotte Haldane. Garden City, NY: Doubleday, 1964, p. 336.

33. Mayke de Jong, "Growing Up in a Carolingian Monastery," *Journal of Medieval History*, vol. 9, 1983, p. 115.

34. Andrew Dickson White, "A History of the Warfare of Science with Theology in Christendom: New Beginnings of Medical Science," n.d. http://abob.libs.uga.edu/book/whitem06.html.

35. Quoted in Ludo J.R. Milis, *Angelic Monks and Earthly Men: Monasticism and Its Meaning to Medieval Society*. Woodridge, UK: Boydell, 1992, p. 58.

36. Anna Comnena, *The Alexiad*, ed. and trans. Elizabeth A. Dawes. London: Routledge, Kegan, Paul, 1928. www.earth-history.com/Europe/eur-alexiad-book-15.htm.

Chapter 5: The Humanists

37. Steven Kreis, "Renaissance Humanism," *The History Guide*, 2004. www.historyguide.org/intellect/humanism.html.

38. Fremantle, *The Age of Faith*, p. 102.

39. Jacob Burckhardt, *The Civilization of the Renaissance in Italy.* New York: Modern Library Classics, 2002, p. 47.

40. Fremantle, *The Age of Faith*, p. 102.

41. Kreis, "Renaissance Humanism."

42. Holmes, *The Oxford Illustrated History of Medieval Europe*, p. 148.

43. H.W. Janson, *History of Art.* New York: Harry N. Abrams, 1963, p. 306.

44. Tuchman, *A Distant Mirror*, p. xix.

Chapter 6: The Emergence of the Nation-State

45. J. Michael Beasley, "Feudalism," *EncycloZine*, 2004. http://encyclo zine.com/Feudalism.

46. Quoted in Edward R. Tannenbaum, *European Civilization Since the Middle Ages.* New York: John Wiley, 1971, p. 41.

For Further Reading

Books

Christopher De Hamel, *Medieval Craftsmen: Scribes and Illuminators*, Toronto: University of Toronto Press, 1992. This book provides an excellent history of the copying and illuminating of medieval texts as well as a variety of color photographs of unusual and beautiful manuscripts.

Anne Fremantle, *The Age of Faith*. New York: Time-Life, 1965. This book focuses on the development of the Christian church in Europe during the Middle Ages. It highlights the role of the church in the lives of knights, the development of the code of chivalry, and the Crusades. Includes an excellent collection of photographs and medieval art.

Frances Gies, *The Knight in History*. New York: Harper & Row, 1984. A straightforward and enjoyable history of the European knight. Gies surveys knighthood as it evolved through the Crusades, examining the effect of the church and of romantic literature on the behavior and status of the mounted warrior.

Frances and Joseph Gies, *Daily Life in Medieval Times*, New York: Black Dog & Leventhal, 1999. An excellent examination of all social classes in medieval Europe; includes beautiful illustrations that complement the text.

Judith Herrin, *A Medieval Miscellany.* London: Viking Studio, 1999. This entertaining book provides over one hundred primary-source entries on a wide variety of fascinating everyday life topics. It fills in many details of medieval life not found in major overviews of this period.

H.W. Janson, *History of Art.* New York: Harry N. Abrams, 1963. This book has been highly regarded for many years as one of the better comprehensive art history books.

Maurice Keen, *Chivalry.* New Haven, CT: Yale University Press, 1984. An excellent academic work exploring the origins, influence, and significance of codes of chivalry and how the codes shaped the role of knights.

Walter Clifford Meller, *A Knight's Life*, London: T. Werner Laurie, 1982. Meller provides a superb account of the variety of responsibilities required of medieval knights. He also exposes the dark side of their profession as sometimes desperate men who trampled on the rights of peasants.

Ludo J.R. Milis, *Angelic Monks and Earthly Men: Monasticism and Its Meaning to Medieval Society*, Woodridge, UK: Boydell, 1992. Milis focuses on the value that medieval monks contributed to European culture as scholars, artists, farmers, and doctors.

Web Sites

Britannia (www.britannia.com/history/ h60.html). This Web site focuses on medieval history in England. It provides a large number of historical articles suitable for young readers along with timelines, current research, and maps.

Chronique (www.chronique.com). This Web site is designed for students as a resource library for hundreds of topics germane to the Middle Ages. Its principal focus is on topics about knights, chivalry, warfare, and tournaments.

The History Channel (www.eyewitnessto history.com). This authorative Web site, provided by the History Channel, offers students a broad range of historical topics from ancient to contemporary history. Included in its offerings are dozens of topics on the Middle Ages all of which include maps and other graphics.

Works Consulted

Books

Thomas Asbridge, *The First Crusade: A New History*, Oxford, UK: Oxford University Press, 2004. Contains a thorough analysis of the motives behind the First Crusade and a detailed chronological account of the events that took place.

Jacob Burckhardt, *The Civilization of the Renaissance in Italy.* New York: Modern Library Classics, 2002. Originally published in 1860, this book was the first to explore the transition of art from the Late Middle Ages to the Renaissance. It remains a classic for its discussions of the changing intellectual climate within the two different periods.

Norman Cantor, ed., *The Medieval Reader.* New York: HarperCollins, 1994. This book contains more than one hundred primary sources from medieval documents.

William R. Cook and Ronald B. Herzman, *The Medieval World View.* Oxford, UK: Oxford University Press, 2004. A narrative of the medieval world and its foundations. Part one presents the classical and biblical background of medieval culture, part two the Early Middle Ages, and part three the Late Middle Ages.

Jean Décarreaux, *Monks and Civilization.* Trans. Charlotte Haldane, Garden City, NY: Doubleday, 1964. This work focuses on the role that monks played in saving and preserving the culture and civilization handed down from the Greeks and Romans that might otherwise have been lost during the Middle Ages.

George Holmes, *The Oxford Illustrated History of Medieval Europe.* Oxford, UK: Oxford University Press, 1990. This work provides an excellent discussion of medieval Europe from 500 to 1500 as well as a fine selection of art photographs.

C.H. Lawrence, *Medieval Monasticism.* London: Longman, 2001. This book is considered one of the best overviews of medieval monasticism. Lawrence is a senior scholar who presents a variety of descriptions and discussions of monks, their place in European history, and their intellectual environments.

G.C. Macauly, ed., *The Chronicles of Froissart.* Trans. Lord Berners. London: Macmillan, 1904. Froissart was a mid-fourteenth-century French traveler who gained fame by writing his memoirs of roving through England, Germany, and France.

Edward R. Tannenbaum, *European Civilization Since the Middle Ages.* New York: John Wiley, 1971. The author traces many of the antecedents of modern European civilization back to the Middle Ages.

Barbara Tuchman, *A Distant Mirror: The Calamitous 14th Century.* New York:

Ballantine, 1978. This book examines daily life during the tragic fourteenth century, which had as its historical backdrop the devastating Black Plague that ravaged all of Europe. It is considered one of the great historical works describing everyday life in medieval Europe for both the peasantry and nobility.

Internet Sources

Stephen Alsford, "History of Medieval Ipswich," 2001. www.trytel.com/~tristan /towns/ipswich6.html.

J. Michael Beasley, "Feudalism," *Encyclo-Zine*, 2004. http://encyclozine.com/ Feudalism.

Scott J. Beem, "The (Not So) Poor Knights of the Temple," Eastern Illinois University, Spring 1996. www.eiu.edu/~historia /1997/knights97.htm.

Chronique: Journal of Chivalry, "Knighting Ceremonies," issue 5. www.chronique. com/Chronique/chrniq05.htm# Chronique5g.

Anna Comnena, *The Alexiad.* Ed. and trans. Elizabeth A. Dawes. London: Routledge, Kegan, Paul, 1928. www.earth-history. com/Europe/eur-alexiad-book-15.htm.

"Crime and Punishment in Elizabethan England," EyeWitness to History, 2001. www.eyewitnesstohistory.com/ punishment.htm.

Dave Etheridge, "Welsh Warfare," Regia Anglorum, 2003. www.regia.org/ welswar.htm.

Paul Halsall, "Boniface VIII, Unam Sanctam, 1302," *Internet Medieval Source Book*, January 1996. www.fordham.edu/ halsall/source/B8-unam.html.

———, "'Feudal' Oaths of Fidelity," *Internet Medieval Source Book*, February 1996. www.fordham.edu/halsall/source /feud-oath1.html.

———, "Fulcher of Chartres: History of the Expedition to Jerusalem," *Internet Medieval Source Book*, December 1997. www.fordham.edu/halsall/source/ fulcher-cde.html.

———, "Peter the Hermit and the Popular Crusade: Collected Accounts," *Internet Medieval Source Book*, December 1997. www.fordham.edu/halsall/source/ peterhermit.html.

Insecta Inspecta World, "Quotes on the Black Death," 2004. www.insecta-inspecta.com/fleas/bdeath/Quotes .html.

Steven Kreis, "European Agrarian Society: Manorialism," *The History Guide*, 2004. www.historyguide.org/ancient/ lec ture22b.html.

———, "Renaissance Humanism," *The History Guide*, 2004. www.historyguide .org/intellect/humanism.html.

Brian R. Price, "Charlemagne the King: A Biography from Will Durant's *Story of Civilization 1950*," *Chronique*, 2000. www.chronique.com/Library/ MedHistory/charlemagne.htm#chess.

Frank E. Smitha, "Warlords of Europe, to 1050," 2000. www.fsmitha.com/h3/ h05eu.htm.

Orderic Vitalis, "The Battle of Hastings According to Orderic Vitalis," in *The Ecclesiastical History of England and Normandy*, vol. 2. Trans. Thomas Forrester. London: Bohn, 1853. www. shsu.edu/~his_ncp/Orderic.html #n11.

Andrew Dickson White, "A History of the Warfare of Science with Theology in Christendom: New Beginnings of Medical Science," n.d. http://abob.libs.uga.edu/bobk/whitem06.html.

Periodicals

E.P. Cheyney, trans., *University of Pennsylvania Translations and Reprints*, vol. 4. Philadelphia: University of Pennsylvania Press, 1898.

Mayke de Jong, "Growing Up in a Carolingian Monastery." *Journal of Medieval History*, vol. 9, 1983.

J.H. Robinson, *University of Pennsylvania Translations and Reprints*, vol. 3. Philadelphia: University of Pennsylvania Press, 1898.

Index

Picture Credits

About the Author

James Barter received his undergraduate degree in history and classics at the University of California in Berkeley, followed by his graduate degree in ancient history and archaeology at the University of Pennsylvania. Mr. Barter has taught history as well as Latin and Greek.

A Fulbright scholar at the American Academy in Rome, Mr. Barter worked on archaeological sites in and around the city as well as Etruscan sites north of Rome and Roman sites in the Naples area. Mr. Barter also has worked and traveled extensively in Greece. Mr. Barter resides in Rancho Santa Fe, California, and lectures throughout the San Diego area.